with winning in mind
the mental management system

of

Olympic Champion
Lanny R. Bassham

Dedication:

To Helen, my reason for winning.

Copyright © 1988 by Lanny Bassham

Printed by X-Press Publications in the USA.

ISBN 0-9619194-2-6

Cover Design by XPress Publications, San Antonio, TX

Contents

What is Mental Management?

Building the Conscious Circle.

Building the Sub-Conscious Circle.

Building the Self Image Circle.

Appendix

Acknowledgments

Special thanks:

To all Olympians. You have been such an inspiration to me.

To those who answered my questions, offered advice and encouraged this effort.

To Gary Anderson, John Foster, John Writer, Margaret Murdock and Lones Wigger Jr. for setting the example. To Bill Pullum, Bill Krilling, the US Army Marksmanship Unit and the NRA for the opportunity.

To all my students, especially Soma Dutta, Eun chul Lee, David Kimes, Ernie Vande Zande, Dr. Rod Fitz-Randolph, Marsha Beasely, Jamie Loesch, Michael & Bentley Storm, Michel Dion, Deborah Ochs, Bob Aylward, Dr. Lindy Hodges, Neal Ward, Paul Coker and Carol, Bryant Dunbar, Elizabeth Bourland, Rolfe Smith, Jeff Kauck, Zal Chitty, Caroline Roberts, Dr. Windell Fairbanks, Dot Martin, Antonio Borja, Chuck Meyer, Dan Morse, Thomas Tu, Roger Withrow, Enid Newton, Shun & Noriko Kosai, Leo Lujan and Dr. Stuart Menn for your friendship, long after the classes ended.

To the Olympic teams of Japan, Australia, Canada, Republic of China and USA for their confidence.

To Rich & Jay and my Amway family for the possible dream.

To Ben & Iris of XPress Publications for the late nights.

To Masaru Fujii for believing more in the system than I.

To Charles M. Stern for helping me to find the words.

To the memory of William and Natalou Bassham for every good day.

Most of all to my wife Helen, my sons Brian & Troy and daughter Heather for making me feel like a champion.

Introduction

I believe that the major reason that people do not read introductions is that they are just too darn long. So I will try to make this one short. In fact, I plan to make this entire book short, to the point and easy to read. It is my desire that you be able to read this book in one sitting and understand what the Mental Management System is all about.

Are you interested in winning or helping others to win? If so, then this book is written for you. I believe there exists a mental system that will speed up the process of getting to the winners circle. I have dedicated the last 20 years of my life to searching out, refining and using this system.

I am well aware that there are many "self improvement" books available. Some are written by psychologists, motivational speakers, religious leaders and business professionals. This one is written by an Olympic champion. What I am and what I teach is the result of winning and losing. I did my apprenticeship in the arena of Olympic competition. My credibility is in my Gold medals and the medals of my students. My goal in this book is to share the winning techniques of Olympic champions with you. I will approach the book as if you and I were talking together. It is the only way I know to teach and achieve results.

Foreword by Masaru Fujii

I first met Lanny Bassham in Wiesbaden, West Germany in the spring of 1970. I was in training in the sport of international rifle shooting at the famous "German Shooting School". Shooters from all over the world come to this facility to enjoy the fantastic shooting ranges, sample the famous food of chef Werner Frankenbach and to learn from each other. It was during such a time that the United States Army Shooting Team visited the shooting school.

There were many "famous" shooters on that team, Lones Wigger, 1964 Olympic Champion, Margaret Murdock, 1966 World Champion, Jack Foster, two time World Champion and Jack Writer, World and Olympic Champion. These were the "heroes" of all shooting students and I spent every minute I could watching and talking to them.

Also on that team was a new shooter from Texas, Lanny Bassham. Then an unknown. I felt drawn to him. Maybe it because he was close to my age and experience. Or maybe it was because we could both feel, even then, that we would become closest of friends in the future. For whatever reason, I spent most of my time with him.

Since that day many things have changed for both of us. I went on to become Japanese National Champion but stopped shooting to develop Heirinkan, a gun shop and shooting supplies center in Tokyo.

Lanny continued to shoot. In 1972 he won the Silver medal in the Olympic Games in Munich Germany. I saw Lanny again the next time in Thun, Switzerland, where he won an unprecedented 15 medals, 8 of them Gold in the 1974 World Shooting Championships. He won the Olympic Gold Medal in 1976 and the World Championships again in 1978.

Since that time Lanny has been teaching MENTAL MANAGEMENT. He has taught thousands of shooters, athletes and business professionals in 10 countries. He is the original developer of the term MENTAL MANAGE-MENT and is the author of best selling video and audio cassette programs. He is a consultant to the Olympic teams of 6 countries in the area of mental training.

I was one of his personal students in 1979 and I have interpreted his teaching in Japanese to more than 100 groups of students. In the last 8 years we have been business partners in Triad Horse Ranch, Dorf Limited of America, an import/export company and in The International Shooting School. Lanny is my international sponsor in the Amway business and I credit his course with helping me to gain financial independence through Amway.

Part I

"What is Mental Management?"

CHAPTER ONE

"It doesn't matter if you win or lose...
Until you lose!"

As a child, I wanted to be a winner and enjoy the rewards of winning. I noticed in elementary school that the kids who won the races were always the happiest. All the others would come up to them and say "That was great, you're super!" but it never happened to me. I never won a race in my life. I wasn't even good enough to be average. You know what they say about average, "The best of the worst or the worst of the best!" Well, I was the worst of the worst.

No one ever comes up to the loser and says "Nice job!" unless it is said in sarcasm. I was always smaller, slower and weaker than the winners. I wanted the recognition but was unable to earn it as an individual. So, I decided to try out for team sports.

I was the last person picked on the baseball team. I got alternate right field. If you have ever played little league baseball, you know that they seldom hit the ball to right field, that's where you put your worst player. And I was the alternate.

I still remember one day, very well. I was in right field and I heard a "funny" crack of the bat. A ball had been hit to me. I had never seen a ball like that before. It was smoking and heading straight for me. I couldn't get out of the way. I had to catch it. I put up my glove, reached for the ball and it hit me right between the eyes. Two runs scored before I could throw it in. The coach was more than a little upset with me.

I remember going home and telling my father that "I'm no good!" He said "No! You are mistaken. There is nothing wrong with you son. You haven't found what you are good at yet. Keep looking. Why not try something where the balls are bigger and easier to catch?"

So the next year I tried out for basketball. The balls were bigger and easier to catch. The coach carefully selected the players and their positions. The guards, center and forwards were selected. I remained on the bench. That's where I sat out the season. Again, I was the last one to play in the games and I was beginning to develop a super low self-image.

I remember one game that I played in particular. The ball got away from one of the other teams players and bounced toward me. This time, I knew exactly what to do. I would take the ball in for an easy lay-up and be a hero for the first time in my life. As I got to the ball, the thought crossed my mind...Is that our goal or is the other one ours? I had forgotten. In my moment of indecision, I accidentally kicked the ball out of play. Again, the coach was not too impressed with me. I was a failure in everything I had tried and I was ready to give up on sports.

People say "It doesn't matter if you win or lose!" But when you lose, it matters a lot. It hurts! The only things that kept me from quitting were the books on the Olympics I had read. I loved the Olympic Games. I wanted, more than anything, to see them in-person. I wanted to meet an Olympic Gold Medalist just once. I thought that if I could stand near one, some of their power would rub off on me.

Then one day a friend of mine told me that he was going to the rifle range. I asked him "Rifle shooting, what is that?"

"It is an Olympic sport" he said. An Olympic Sport? I was interested.

"Tell me, how strong do you have to be to be a rifle shooter?"

"You don't have to be strong!" he said.

"Tell me, how tall do you have to be to be a rifle shooter?"

"You don't have to be tall!"

3

"Tell me, how fast do you have to be to be a rifle shooter?"

"You don't understand." he replied. "You don't have to be tall or strong or fast. All you have to do is stand still."

"Great!" I exclaimed. "An Olympic sport where all you have to do is learn to stand still. I can do that! I've had lots of practice in the dugout and on the bench. At last, I've found something I can be good at." That was the beginning of my shooting career.

My father saw that this might be a way for me to develop some self confidence. He encouraged me and bought me the best equipment. He became interested in the sport as well. We practiced together, went to matches together and became a team. You see, Dad never played baseball or football either. My father and I became best friends on the rifle range.

I don't remember much about growing up. I was too busy training. When all the other kids went to movies, I practiced. I trained an average of five hours a day, five days a week for ten years before I made my first Olympic team. I shot on the high school and college rifle teams. I would go into school early and train. Then I would train again before going home. The weekends were for matches

4

or all day training. I received a business degree in college, but I majored in shooting. After many hours, I thought there must be another way that did not require so much time and effort to succeed. I did not have a Mental Management System then. If I had, I could have done better on half the effort and half the time. But, I am getting ahead of the story.

I remember my first Olympiad in 1972 in Munich, Germany. My team mate, Jack Writer was the best shooter in the world. He had won all three Olympic World Cups and was the "hand's on" favorite to win the Gold. Jack's only problem was me. I occasionally beat him in training. And the occasion was occurring more and more often the closer we got to Olympic day. I thought I was going to win the Gold medal and Jack would take the Silver.

Olympic day arrived. I was technically equal to Jack, but I had not considered the effect of the OLYMPIC PRESSURE.

When the match started, I began to shake. I shot nine after nine. I was so scared that I lost the match in my first ten shots due to a poor mental performance. At that time, I felt like my world had ended. I had failed my country, my family and myself. Ten years of training had not fully prepared me to win the Gold. I lacked the mental skills. Jack Writer was the champion that day. I managed to win the Silver.

Now don't get me wrong. The Silver medal is ten times better than the Bronze and the Bronze is ten times better than no medal at all. But, to my way of thinking, the Silver is the closest thing you can get to the Gold Medal and STILL LOSE! I knew that I had to come back to win in 1976. I also knew, that to do that, I needed a new mental game.

I wanted to take a course in mental training. But, in 1972, there were no mental training seminars. In fact, the only way to learn how to cope with the mental stress of the Olympics, was to question other Olympic Gold medalists, on their mental techniques. That is exactly what I did. Over the next two years, I spent an average of five hours a day gathering information on the mental aspect of sport. I interviewed champions, asking questions like: "What do you think about when you are performing?" and "What makes you able to win when others fail?"

At last, my shooting started to come together like pieces of a puzzle. In 1974, I established the U.S. National Record at 1179/1200, which stood for more than fourteen years. In the World Shooting Championships in Switzerland, I won eight Gold medals for my country.

In many ways I had become a different person. When my mental attitude changed, I was more confident and in control. I changed my self image. My habits and attitudes were that of a winner. I had developed a system to control the mental aspects of my performance, a Mental Management System. Finally, winning became a habit. In 1976 in Montreal, Canada my lifelong dream came true... The Olympic Gold Medal. Then, two years later, I repeated as World Champion in Seoul, Korea.

I began teaching the Mental Management System to athletes, shortly after the Olympics. I have given seminars on four continents and the system has been translated into more than a half dozen languages. I have as clients the Olympic teams of Japan, Australia, India, Canada, the Republic of China and USA. The system works for all sports, such as golf, tennis, soccer, gymnastics as well as all shooting sports including archery. I have had the pleasure of presenting the Mental Management System to business professionals such as doctors, attorneys, teachers, accountants, directors of sales and even the United States Secret Service.

CHAPTER TWO

"Why Winners Win."

In my more than 25 years in competition, I have been both a participant and a winner. I can tell you frankly, it is much more satisfying to win. I think everyone knows that. A fact that is not so widely known is that 95% of all winning is done by only 5% of the participants.

What makes the 5% different? It's not their size, color, nationality, or economic situation. It's not anything they are born with, unless we admit we are all born with the seeds of greatness within us. It is my observation, after competing against and teaching the world's best, that the only thing that separates the winners from the others is the way they think. Winners are convinced they will finish first. The others hope to finish first.

An example of this difference is the great Olympic shooting champion from England, Malcolm Cooper. We were in Seoul, Korea in 1978 for the World Shooting Championships. Malcolm was favored to win the world title, in the standing position, as he held the world record. Just before the competition was to begin he said "I'm going to win today!" It wasn't said in a bragging tone. The man was just convinced he was going to win. Then he discovered that his rifle was damaged and he had to borrow another shooter's rifle for the match. Then I heard him say, "Wouldn't it be something special to win this match with a borrowed rifle. I'm going to do it!" And that is exactly what he did, setting the world record in the process! You see, he "expected" to win. Therein lies the difference. I am not saying that everyone who expects to win will always win. What I am saying is that "if one does not expect to win, he has no chance at all of winning."

Another example of one who expected to win is archer Darrell Pace. I first met Darrell in 1976 at the Olympics. At 5 feet 10 inches tall and only 115 pounds, Darrell looked like anything but an Olympic athlete. Yet at the tender age of 19, he was already World Champion and the world record holder. I spent a lot of time with Darrell in Montreal. We would meet together in the evenings, after our training sessions. I was fascinated by Darrell's bold attitude of confidence. He was convinced that there was absolutely no possibility that he could loose the Gold medal. He referred to the Gold as "My medal." He would say, "I wonder where they are keeping my medal." "Everyone is after my medal but they cannot take it from me!" He had already won the Gold medal in his mind.

I asked him why he was so certain he would win. Darrell's answer, "I am more committed to mental training than any of my competitors!"

I kept thinking about Darrell as my event drew near. He had helped to reinforce many of my own attitudes on winning. On the day of my event, as I prepared my equipment to compete, I saw Darrell sitting next to my wife, Helen in the spectator area. "He has come to watch me win," I thought. The time for talking was over. Now, it was a time for winning. We both won our Gold medal that year.

Darrell Pace and Edwin Moses are the only Americans who won Olympic Gold medals in both '76 and '84.

Last evening as I began this chapter, I received a phone call from Deborah Ochs, a student of mine, saying that she had qualified for the U.S. Olympic team for Seoul. She was calling from the home of Darrell Pace, who had just made his fourth Olympic team. He is going after "his medal" once again.

I believe that the expectation of winning comes from an internal feeling the champion has concerning his performance. He is in harmony with the idea that his expectation and his performance will be equal. In recent years, I have spent most of my time studying what makes champions consistent winners. I feel certain that most people do not win, because they simply lack a mental system to control their performance under stress. Once this system is in place, winning is possible.

What is your game? Golf? Archery? Tennis? Football? Soccer? Shooting? Sales? Parenting? Management? Coaching? Teaching? What percentage of what you do is mental? What percentage is pure physical or technique? I have asked that question to hundreds of Olympic athletes and business persons. They all have answered 80 to 90 percent mental!

Performance is 90 percent mental.

To control performance, especially in high level competition you need a system. The system that I use and teach is called the Mental Management System.

"MENTAL MANAGEMENT is the process of maximizing the probability of having a consistent mental performance, under pressure, on demand."

I wanted a system that would work all the time, in competition, under pressure. This is such a system. You will never again have the excuse that you could not win, because you were not mentally prepared, after you read this book.

An outstanding performance is powerful! Also, an outstanding performance is easy! Only poor performance is plagued by frustration and extra effort. Think about it.

When do you expend the greatest effort, when you are doing well or when you are doing poorly. When you are playing golf well, the ball goes straight down the fairway. You do not have to chase it into the rough. You do not spend time looking for the ball. When you play well you are balanced and in harmony with your efforts. When I won the Olympics, the actual performance seemed easy for me because I was balanced in my three mental processes: the Conscious Mind, the Sub-Conscious Mind and the Self Image.

The Mental Management System, therefore, is concerned with the understanding of these processes, developing them to their full potential and keeping a careful balance between them.

These mental processes are, in their most basic form:

The Conscious Mind: The source of thoughts...our mental pictures. The Conscious Mind controls all of your senses; seeing, hearing, smelling, tasting, and touching. It is what you picture or think about.

The Sub-Conscious Mind: The source of your skills and power to perform. All good performance is accomplished sub-consciously. We develop skill through repetition of conscious thought until it becomes automatically done by the Sub-Conscious mind.

The Self Image: It makes you "act like you!" The Self Image is the total of your habits and your attitudes. Your performance and your Self Image are always equal.

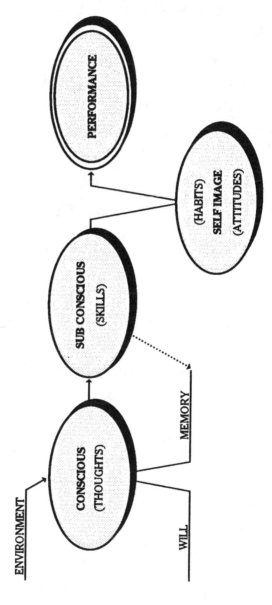

CHAPTER THREE

"THE TRIAD"
Principles of Mental Management

Gravity is a proven principle of physics. We all feel the pull of the earth on us. Just as there are principles of physical motion, there are also principles of success.

The Principles of Mental Management govern how the mind works. These principles are concepts, common to winners, that have stood the test of time. They work for all people, all the time and are applicable to sports performance, business success and personal development. Remember, success is not an accident. It follows a set course and these principles are the boundaries of its path.

Principle of MENTAL MANAGEMENT Number 1

If you are picturing something positive, it is impossible, at the same time, to picture something negative and vice versa.

Why is this mental picture important? Because, you have to make a choice. It is impossible to picture winning and losing at the same time. You are either picturing something that will help you or something that will hurt you. And, if you constantly control the image in your mind in a positive manner, it is <u>impossible</u> to have a concentration error and a poor performance.

I had a baseball coach once who always told me, "Whatever you do Bassham, don't strike out." What do you picture when I say "Don't strike out!" It is impossible to think about hitting the ball if you are picturing striking out.

In Olympic level shooting, I found that it was impossible to concentrate on shooting a ten and count my score at the same time. If my thoughts centered on score, my performance fell. I had to keep my mental picture centered on performing the shot.

<u>Principle of MENTAL MANAGEMENT Number 2</u>

"What you say is not important. What you cause others to picture is critical!"

This is the fundamental principle of successful communication.

It is not important what you say, it is only important what you cause someone to picture. When the coach said, "Whatever you do Bassham, DON'T STRIKE OUT!" I pictured striking out. He set me up for failure by the way he

16

talked to me. If he had said "GO STRIKE OUT!" it would have had the same effect on me. He should have said. "Bassham, HIT THE BALL!"

When you begin anything, whether it be piano lessons or your first day on the golf course, good performance seems difficult. It seems difficult because you are trying to do everything consciously. Most things, such as playing music, or golf requires you to do many things at the same time. As the Conscious mind can only do one thing at a time, the lessons, in the beginning, are very frustrating. The Conscious mind needs assistance. It receives this backup from the second mental process...The Sub-Conscious Mind.

The Sub-Conscious Mind

The Sub-Conscious mind is where your skills are developed. After that first piano lesson, things begin to get easier as you develop skill through practice. Skill is defined as doing something consciously long enough for the process to become automated by the Sub-Conscious mind.

Unlike the Conscious mind, the Sub-Conscious can do many things at once. In fact, your brain is like a huge computer. Just how many separate functions can be handled by the Sub-Conscious simultaneously is hard to measure, but it may be in the millions. That is why we need to per-

17

form in the Sub-Conscious mode, rather than the Conscious. It is far more powerful. A rifle shooter, who has Sub-Conscious trigger control, will activate the trigger when the sights are aligned. A shooter who Consciously activates the trigger, will most probably move the rifle as he shoots, thereby throwing the shot off.

Principle of MENTAL MANAGEMENT Number 3

"The Sub-Conscious Mind is the source of all mental power."

This is good news and bad news. The good news is that each of us has within us the power to achieve anything we desire. The bad news is that we are only using 5% of the power available to us. Why do we use so little? To use more takes both knowledge and effort. Few people know how and even fewer are willing to put out the effort. Those that do are consistently among the winners.

Good performance looks easy. One of the most often watched sports is gymnastics. These fine athletes make their very difficult sport "look" easy. I remember the first time I tried to pull myself up on the rings. That day I gained a great respect for the strength needed to be a gymnast. Their skill comes from years of training. The routines are so well learned that they are Sub-Consciously automated. I once asked a gymnast on the US team what he thought about when he performed. He answered, "I try to feel the flow of the routine. I do not want to think that any element is especially difficult or dangerous while performing."

You perform best when you allow your well trained Sub-Conscious to do the work. The Conscious mind can over ride the Sub-Conscious. When this happens performance almost always deteriorates. Sleep is a Sub-Conscious action. You may attempt to over ride the Sub-Conscious by Consciously attempting to make yourself GO TO SLEEP NOW. You will probably be up most of the night.

Conscious over ride is a major problem for Olympic athletes on Olympic day. Instead of trusting the Sub-Conscious mind to perform, athletes try extra hard to do well. Conscious override is the result. You tighten up. You slow down. Off your rhythm, your performance drops. You must allow the Sub-Conscious to do the work. Trust in your ability. Let it Flow...

<u>Principle of MENTAL MANAGEMENT Number 4</u>

"The Sub-Conscious moves you to do whatever the Conscious mind is picturing."

When my daughter was 9 years old, I asked her to carry a cup of coffee to a guest in our house. Then I said,

"Don't spill it!" Now, that was the wrong thing to tell her. When she spilled the coffee, I should not have been surprised. After all, I put the idea in her mind. It was my error, not hers. You see, when you say "Don't spill the coffee!" what picture is created in the Conscious mind? I picture spilling the coffee. The Sub-Conscious moves you to do whatever the conscious mind is picturing and it is picturing spilling the coffee."

It is the same in sports. There are only four seconds left in the game, time for only one more play. A touchdown is needed to win. The coach calls for his best fullback to carry the ball. He explains the play.

"Now young man, you are our only hope to win this game. I want you to go in there and and take the hand-off from the quarterback and run in for the touchdown. You can do it!"

In goes the fullback and explains the play to the quarterback who says, "That's great. We are going to win as long as YOU DON'T FUMBLE!"

Being positive is our only hope. Positive pictures, demand positive results from the Sub-Conscious. If we think negatively, we will have to expect negative results.

The mind is like a submarine. The Conscious mind is the periscope. The Sub-Conscious is the engine and the Self Image is the throttle of that engine. The Sub-

Conscious is always asking the Conscious mind what it sees. Then it launches the boat in that direction. The speed is determined by the Self Image.

"The Self Image"

The Self Image makes you "act like you!" You have "your special way" of behaving.

Some people like to get up early in the morning.

Some people like to get up late.

Some people think they are good in math.

Some people are terrified by speaking before a group.

Some people hope they can win.

Some people expect to win.

We all have our own way of behaving. The sad thing is that most people believe they cannot change their behavior pattern. They believe that the way they act and react cannot be altered. In fact, we are all changing constantly. The direction of that change can either be determined <u>by</u> you or <u>for</u> you. The choice is yours.

You cannot change your height, but you can change how high you get!

Principle of MENTAL MANAGEMENT Number 5

"The Self Image and performance are always equal. In order to change your performance, you must first change your Self Image."

Your Self Image is like the throttle of the submarine. It controls the speed and distance you can go. We all limit ourselves by our Self Image. For example, it is not like me to drive my car ninety miles an hour. In fact, if I get just a few miles over the speed limit, my Self Image makes me feel uncomfortable, until I slow down. It's not like me to drive fast, therefore I don't.

Another example is the car salesman who averages selling four cars a month. If he goes the first three weeks without selling a car, his Self Image makes him work harder to sell four the last week of the month. Also, if he sells four the first week, the Self Image will slow him down the rest of the month. It is just not like him to sell more than four cars a month.

We all have comfort zones. It is like us to operate within them. As long as we are in the zone, our Self Image is content to leave us alone. If, however, we start scoring lower than our limit, the Self Image will provide us with extra power to improve until we are back within the zone. Likewise, if we start scoring better than our comfort zone, the Self Image tends to slow us down until we are, once again, back in the zone. Change the zone and change the performance. To change the comfort zone, we must change the Self Image. That brings us to the next principle of MENTAL MANAGEMENT.

Principle of MENTAL MANAGEMENT Number 6

"You can replace the Self Image you have with the Self Image you want and therefore, permanently change performance!"

You can replace the income you have with the income you want.

You can replace the score you have with the score you want.

You can replace the YOU you have with the YOU you want.

The problem for most of us is that we are aware that something has to change for our lives to improve, but we want the change to be in someone else or with something else and not from within us.

If only my friends would change.

If only my boss would change.

If only the dollar was higher against the yen.

If only another political party were in power.

If only my wife would change her mind.

If only... If only... NOTHING IS GOING TO CHANGE UNTIL YOU CHANGE FIRST.

Change is a difficult challenge to face. Most of us think we are pretty good the way we are and we resist change. Besides, it is easier for us to place the burden to change on someone else, then it's no longer our problem. It takes effort to change.

The Self Image resists change. Sometimes the Self Image speaks to you. When your alarm clock sounds early in the morning, you hear, "You're tired. Don't get up! Let's stay in bed today, call in sick." Your Self Image is the area of your inner self that conveys ideas to you. It tells you things like, "What makes you think you are going to win? You've never won before." Or "We are going to do whatever it takes to win this time!"

Principle of MENTAL MANAGEMENT Number 7

The Principle of Balance: "When the Conscious, Sub-Conscious and Self Image are all balanced and working together, good performance is easy."

When the Conscious, Sub-Conscious and Self Image are in balance and working as a team, this is called the TRIAD STATE. In this state, you work smoothly, efficiently, and seemingly effortlessly toward your goal. It's a wonderful feeling and has been experienced by almost everyone at one time or another. The problem is that we do not experience it often enough.

The key is to experience it under pressure, on demand. Therein lies the challenge. Some of us score well in practice, but not in the competition. We desire to have consistent mental performance all the time. That is the definition of MENTAL MANAGEMENT – the process of improving the probability of having a consistent mental performance, under pressure, on demand.

CHAPTER FOUR

"The Balance of Power"

In the Triad State, one is balanced and in harmony and great performances can become a reality. It is this balance that produces power.

If a baseball player is in the TRIAD STATE, he is concentrating on getting a hit, has trained so well that he is swinging Sub-Consciously and has the attitude that it is "like me" to hit the ball. The result is a hit.

If a salesman is in the TRIAD STATE, he is concentrating on solving his client's problem through the sale of his product, has practiced his presentation enough so that it is Sub-Consciously done. He has the attitude that it is "like me" to make the sale. The result is an order.

One can demonstrate the TRIAD STATE by the use of the model in figure 4.1.

In this model, all the processes are of equal size and the TRIAD STATE effect occurs. Good performance seems easy. Perhaps you have experienced this feeling, when nothing can go wrong. When you are balanced, you love

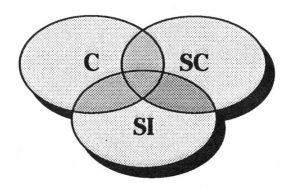

Figure 4.1

your sport and have a minimum of challenges. You perform well and everything seems easy.

In fact, you cannot be beaten when you are in the Triad State, unless you face an opponent that is also in the Triad State with superior ability.

However, often we are out of balance. And the following results (see figure 4.2) are common.

When we begin any new activity, whether it be a new job, business, musical instrument or sport, we are out of balance. We have good Conscious focus on the activity, but we have not yet developed Sub-Conscious skill. Also, our Self Image is such that we are "beginners" and cannot perform well. In this condition, the new activity seems dif-

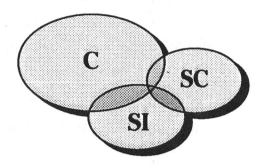

Figure 4.2

ficult. Remember that first day in piano lessons? If we practice properly and we are encouraged, our Sub-Conscious and Self Image circles will grow to match the Conscious circle and we will be in balance.

Often times, however, something like the following figure happens. See figure 4.3.

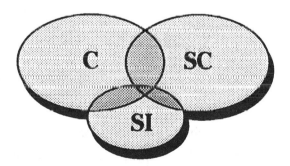

Figure 4.3

This is an example of a person who had trained for many years and has acquired exceptional skill, but for whatever the reason the Self Image has not grown sufficiently. Someone who scores well in training but scores much lower in the competition meets this description. This person has all the qualifications to become a success but as yet does not believe in himself. In order to perform well, this person must improve his Self Image circle.

Unfortunately, many people in this situation, do not recognize that they must work on their Self Image. They work, instead, on their Sub-Conscious skill, becoming even more out of balance.

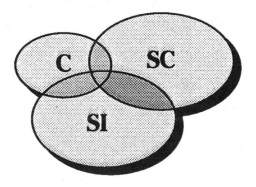

Figure 4.4

This person is well trained and has a good Self Image, but is not concentrating on his activity. He is like the "gun-slinger" of the old west, who would blow into his barrel after each shot. Then one day he aimed to blow and is shot instead.

One must always keep one's Conscious mind on the activity at hand or careless error will result. This person must develop better concentration skills or a stronger goal so that the Conscious circle will be in balance with the others.

Figure 4.5

Overconfidence is a trait the champion must avoid if he is to stay on top for very long. Here is a person that has an oversize Self Image for the level of Sub-Conscious skill he possesses. He always boasts that he will win but falls short because of a lack of proper preparation. He feels that he will win because he is wonderful, not because he is prepared. There is nothing wrong with having a big Self Image as long as you are willing to balance it with an equally large level of Conscious and Sub-Conscious skill.

The key point is to learn how to make your circles larger and at the same time keep them in balance. If you have balanced growth, you have an automatic performance increase without stress and frustration. That is everyone's aim. We all know that to become better requires effort and time. What we least want is to spend a lot of time and energy and not progress.

Every time I notice a frustrated athlete, I wonder, "Which process is out of balance?"

If you just cannot seem to move ahead in your sport or business, ask yourself these questions:

"Am I out of balance?"

"Am I concentrating on my goals?"

"Do I really posses the skills to do my job well?"

"Do I need more training?"

"Is it like me to do this job or do I need to change something about me to do the work?"

We are all out of balance at one time or another in our lives. To get back in the Triad we must cause our process circles to expand. In our next section we will study principles, tools and techniques to increase each of these circles.

32

CHAPTER FIVE

"The Mental Management Goal Setting System"

One thing I have noticed that separates the top 5% that win from the other 95% that just play, is the habit of setting goals. Most people never set them. No surprise here. This is common knowledge. Every major corporation sets goals. Every government sets goals. Every builder who builds, has a blueprint. Every banker has a written contract on how the borrower is going to pay back each loan. But... it seems that only the super successful ever bother to set personal goals and plan their work.

Recently, my 17 year old asked me if I would buy him a Ferrari automobile for his high school graduation. I think he knew my answer as he asked the question. I took the opportunity to show my son how to set goals by asking him some important questions.

"Son, exactly what is your goal?"

"I want you to buy me a new red Ferrari sports car with brown leather seats."

"When do you want it?"

Part II

"Building the Conscious Circle"

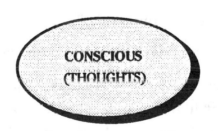

"Graduation day."

"Why should I do that?"

"It would make your son very happy."

"What do you suppose would be the obstacles to my getting you that car?"

"$125,000 more than you have in the bank?"

"The only way I have of obtaining that kind of cash is to sell our home and all our property. Can you think of any other way?"

"No, Sir."

"Son, do you think the joy I would receive in getting you that car is worth my selling our home?"

"No Dad!"

"You are a smart young man!"

"Thanks, could I have a drum set instead?"

Are your goals just pipe dreams? Are your goals set too high or not high enough. There is a process I have learned from my Olympic training experience that you can use to set your goals just right. I call it the Mental Management Goal Setting System.

Step Number 1.

"Decide Exactly What you Want!"

Find goals that excite you. You must be specific. The more you can identify exactly what you want, the better your chances of obtaining them.

Step Number 2.

"Decide When You Want It!"

Putting a time limit on your goals, helps you to better formulate a plan to achieve them. If your goal was to save $1000 in ten years, you could do that by putting about a quarter a day in the bank. If you change the time limit to $1000 in one month, the plan would have to change.

Step Number 3.

"List the Pay Value!"

Why do you want the goal? List all the reasons that are important to you for getting the goal. The first rule here is to make certain that the goal you set is big enough to be exciting for you. If it is not exciting, you will not do anything to change your habits or attitudes. It will just not be worth it.

Also the goal must be your goal, not the goal of another. Is the pay value personally of value to you. I had a friend in college, a pre-dentistry major, that did not want to be a dentist. His grandfather and father were dentists, and the family expected him to join the profession. He hated school.

If the pay value is not personal, you will not act on your plan. A few years ago, my wife told me that she needed new bedroom furniture. She knew exactly what she wanted. Helen provided me with the exact brand, style and number of pieces she desired.

"Helen, this is expensive stuff. Where am I supposed to get the money to pay for it?" I said.

"You'll think of something!"

Several weeks passed and I had completely forgotten about the furniture. I didn't want new bedroom furniture, Helen did. It didn't bother me that the drawers stuck, the finish was scratched and the mirror had a small crack in it. I just kept the light out in the bedroom. When Helen asked how the project was coming along, I said, "I'm working on it."

The next weekend I returned from doing a seminar out of town and Helen picked me up from the airport. She presented me with several bright new twenty dollar bills.

"Helen, where did you get this money?"

"Remember, what you tell your students, to get what you want you have to get rid of what you don't want. So, I sold our bedroom furniture."

Suddenly, I had pay value. I was the only man I knew with his mattress on the floor and his underwear in cardboard boxes. Helen's goal became my goal. I had to get that new furniture. But I didn't have any money.

That weekend I attended a shotgun match. I overheard a conversation concerning furniture and guns. I met a man that traded new furniture for used guns. In fifteen minutes, a deal was negotiated, new bedroom furniture for a mental management seminar and my shotgun.

Step Number 4.

"Ask Yourself, 'Why Don't I Have the Goal Now?' "

Again, you must be specific! What must you do to reach your goals? What habits and attitudes must you change to reach your goal? Remember, nothing is going to get better until you get better. You must change! What must you change? How much additional time must you invest?

Step Number 5.

"Ask...What is your plan to get your goal?"

The difference between a wish and a goal is that a goal has a written plan. Wishes often do not come true. Goals with written plans are almost always reached. In Step Number 4 you identified several reasons why you were unable to meet you goal. Set out a written plan to over-come each obstacle. Now it is clear just what price you are going to have to pay for the attainment of the goal.

Step Number 6.

"Ask yourself...Is the prize worth the price?"

This is the most important step in the goal setting pro-cess. Ask yourself "Is the pay value worth the price I have to pay for it?" If the answer is positive, chances are your goal and plan are correct. If the plan and pay value do not match, you must change something. Maybe you need to change the goal, the time limit or perhaps the plan.

Step Number 7.

"Schedule Your Plan."

One thing that we often fail to remember, is that scheduling is a vital part of the planning process. Put your plans on a calender. I use both a large monthly calender on my office wall and a day planner that I carry with me. If it is not scheduled, it will not get done.

When my daughter was 8 years old, she overheard me saying, "If it is on the calender it will be done." The next day I saw marked on my calender in crayon the words, "Buy Heather a stuffed animal." What do you think I did?

Step Number 8.

"Start Now!"

You are now ready to go. Begin right away. Do not hesitate. Execute the first step of your plan now. Put out high quality effort, consistently over time and there is nothing you cannot do.

Step Number 9.

"Never Reach a Goal Without First Setting Another One!"

The day I received my Olympic Gold Medal was both wonderful and traumatic for me. The award ceremony was great. Hearing my country's National Anthem being played while the flag was raised high in front of me was the best of feelings! However, later that day, I had an unexpected experience. I suffered severe depression and I didn't know why. My wife Helen, recognized the problem and helped me to understand that I had lost my goal. I had not goal set beyond the Olympic Games and I was momentarily without direction. Once I set a new goal, I was again at peace.

Step Number 10.

"Never, Never Quit!"

In 1970, before I developed the Mental Management

System, I set a goal to win the national title in the Air Rifle event. I thought that it would take a 380/400 to win. In the match, I was down nineteen points with three shots left to go. I shot a nine. Now I had to shoot two tens, I figured, to win. I shot another nine. I was down below 380. I rationalized that I could not win, so I mentally gave up. I quickly put up the rifle and shot an eight. I finished with a 377. That year the National Championship went for a 378. Had I been persistent, I would have won the title. Stay with your plan until it is finished.

CHAPTER SIX

"Reinforcement"

Concentration is nothing more than the control of one's picture. Remember the Sub-Conscious, with all it's power, moves you to do whatever the conscious mind is picturing. If you can control the picture, you can control the performance. Your conscious picture is formed from what you think about, talk about and write about.

Principle of MENTAL MANAGEMENT Number 8

The Principle of Reinforcement: "The more we think about, talk about or write about something happening, we improve the probability of that thing happening!"

This is my favorite principle of MENTAL MANAGEMENT. Every time we think about something happening, we improve the probability that it will happen. Be careful what you think about.

What do you picture? Every time you worry, you improve the probability that what you are worrying about will happen. If you are worrying about scoring badly on an exam, the Sub-Conscious, with all its power, will move you to score badly. It is not what you want, but it is what you

41

will get if you continue to think this way. What you must do is picture scoring well.

Be careful of what you talk about. Two shooters meet after a match, shooter A and shooter B. Shooter A asks, "How did you shoot?" B says, "I did terrible. I shot three nines in a row. Two were out the left for wind and the other one came because I held too long." Now, shooter B has just improved the probability of having nines the same way in the future because he is thinking and talking about his mistakes.

The sad thing is that because shooter A is listening to shooter B, he is also improving the chance that he will have B's problems in the future. Be careful who you listen to. Do not spend time listening to the problems of others or you will soon inherit their problems.

I remember some time ago presenting a seminar to Olympic shooters. I was asked the question, "Mr. Bassham, in the 1978 World Championships, you shot a 598/600 to win a medal. What happened on those two nines?" I answered, "Do you really want to know? Do you want to know how I got nines. That will not help you. You don't want to know how I got two nines. What you should be asking is how I got fifty-eight tens. Besides, I can't remember how I got the nines. I do not reinforce bad shots by remembering them."

What you want to talk about are your good shots. By doing that you improve the probability that you will have more good shots in the future.

Be sure to write down what you want. For several years, I have had the pleasure of teaching the Canadian Olympic Shooting Team. In one of the seminars, I remember telling the shooters that it has always been my habit to write down my goals as if they have already been accomplished. At the break, one of their lady pistol shooters and I were visiting about her goal to become the 1984 Olympic pistol champion. I suggested that she write down daily, "I am the 1984 Olympic pistol champion!" Only two things could happen, either she would attain her goal or she would stop writing down the goal.

In the Olympics in 1984, this shooter, Linda Thom, tied for the gold medal with another friend of mine, the USA National Champion, Ruby Fox. In the shoot off, Linda was victorious, winning the Gold medal. Later, we met and talked about her victory. She told me that she knew she was going to win the shoot off, because she had never missed a day, writing her goal in her diary. Writing your goal, improves the probability that it will be attained.

Be careful not to complain. I often hear people, in business as well as sport, complaining about their circumstance. Complaining is negative reinforcement. I teach my students not to reinforce a bad shot by getting angry. Do not reinforce a bad day at the office by complaining to your spouse. Remember anything that you did well each day. Fill your thoughts only with your best performances and you cannot help but be successful!

Prediction- Reinforcement in Advance.

People tend to perform in the same way that we expect them to perform. There is a technique that I call "Prediction," that is useful in increasing performance. It is a complement, given in advance of a future action. My father once told me that to obtain what you want you must first provide someone else what they want. Herein is the essence of the prediction technique. Here are some examples.

I receive exceptional service at my local bank. Although, I am certain that the employees at my bank attempt to provide fine service to everyone, I feel certain that I receive special treatment. Why? I use the prediction technique. From the very first day I opened my account, I have consistently complemented everyone in the bank, in advance, for their excellent treatment of my business. In return, I have received exceptional treatment. I said to the teller, "I appreciate you. You always have a smile for me when I come in the bank and you're really good at your job." The tellers have told me that they rarely receive this kind of treatment from all the bank's customers and that they look forward to my coming to the bank. I seldom have to stand in a long line. When I come into the bank someone says, "Mr. Bassham, I'll open this station for you."

Prediction can be harmful, if used incorrectly. Eunchul Lee is the Asian Shooting Champion from Korea and has been a student at my International Shooting School. Several years ago, after training at my school, Eunchul was shooting once again with the Korean team in a competition in Mexico City. The Korean coach told me that he did not like Eunchul's prone position. He also informed me that Eunchul's attitude was poor.

I had worked with Eunchul for over a year, this coach had only met him the week before. This coach wanted to win so much that he put excessive pressure on his shooters and they became as tight as a drum. Eunchul is, by nature, a very friendly and outgoing young man. His coach took this to indicate that he was not serious about his shooting. I told the Korean coach that I respected his ability and that I would look into his criticisms of my shooter as soon as we returned to the USA.

It was fortunate that Eunchul had finished his match before his coach could tell him about his poor attitude and incorrect prone position. Eunchul Lee won most of the medals for Korea, including a gold in prone. Later the Korean coach came to me, apologized and asked me to look at the prone positions of his other shooters.

I recall one incident where I was the object of the prediction technique. My wife and I had owned an Amway distributorship for about a year when we were introduced by our upline Dr. Tom Zizic to a Mr. Chuck Strehli. Chuck and his wife Jean are Crown Ambassador Direct Distributors, Amway's highest level of recognition. Tom introduced us this way.

"Chuck, I would like for you to meet Lanny and Helen Bassham. They will become new Direct Distributors in August of this year."

"Congratulations," Chuck said, "I'm always pleased to meet new Directs. Did I hear correctly? You will reach the Direct level in August?"

"That's right!" I replied. Until that moment Helen and I had never thought of ourselves as making the Direct level. By August that year, we were new Directs. Tom's prediction came true.

When prediction is implemented, everyone wins. You feel great using the technique. The person you are talking to gets a lift, and the results make everyone feel wonderful.

Prediction is an attitude that says "I expect exceptional service because you are an exceptional person."

Praise- Reinforcement After the Fact.

Praise good performance and the good performance will repeat. If praising others becomes your habit, you will soon become surrounded by competent people that love to work with you.

The teachers, in our local school, are exceptionally considerate of my children. I called the school office to set an appointment with each of my child's teachers. When I met them they would ask, "Mr. Bassham, why did you wish to see me. Is there a problem?"

"I just wanted to meet you and say that you are one of the most considerate teachers in the school. I am delighted that my child has the opportunity to be in your class. I expect, now that we have met, you will not hesitate to give me a call if there is anything that we can do to aid our child in school."

Teachers are not used to hearing good news. It really makes their day when a parent calls in to complement rather than complain. How much better would you do your job, if you were praised more often?

Praise is an attitude that says "I recognize exceptional service because you're an exceptional person."

47

CHAPTER SEVEN

"REHEARSAL...The most versatile mental tool."

A mental tool is a technique you can use to improve your mental performance. A good mental tool will work all the time, for every one, at least to some degree. The most often used mental tool among athletes is rehearsal. It has many other names, such as mental imagery and visualization. I like the term rehearsal because it is easy to relate to. If you were in a play or a show, you would know what the term rehearsal meant. It is practicing for the real thing.

In mental rehearsal you are picturing what you want to see happen, before you actually perform. You go over, in your mind exactly how you want your performance to be done. In rifle shooting, you picture holding the rifle, looking through the sights, centering the target and firing the shot in the ten ring. In business, you picture every step of a critical task and the desired result. The more vivid the picture the better the outcome. The more often you do rehearsal, the better the chance for success because of the Principle of Reinforcement.

Uses for Mental Rehearsal...

"Use Number 1- Mental Practice"

Rehearsal is mental practice. For the rifle shooter, it has great advantages. First, you are mentally duplicating everything you do when you are on the range, without going there. You do not have to buy bullets, targets or wear out your equipment. You do not have to clean up the range or clean your rifle when you finish. And it's cheap! It costs absolutely nothing! And you can do it anytime. You rehearse only good performances, so there is no negative reinforcement. Mental practice is a bargain.

You can imagine far more than you think you can achieve. If you consistently rehearse, imagination becomes reality.

I had been shooting good kneeling scores, approaching the national record of 396. I wanted to set the record at 400, a perfect score. I had never actually fired a 400 even in training.

I vividly rehearsed shooting the first 100, then another and another. I visualized that last ten shots. Ten. Ten. Ten. Ten. Ten. Only five more to go. Ten. Ten. Ten. Then the realization set in that I was above the record. I rehearsed hearing a voice say, "That's OK, I do this all the time." Then I imagined easily shooting two more tens. "Another 400, that's like me!"

I rehearsed this sequence several times a day for two months. In my first competition since beginning the rehearsal, I started with a 100 kneeling. My next two scores also 100s. I began my last series with Ten, Ten, Ten, Ten, Ten. Only five more to go. Ten. Ten. Ten. Then reality set in. I was above the record. I heard a voice say, "That's OK, I do this all the time." I shot two additional tens, setting the national record at a perfect 400.

Principle of MENTAL MANAGEMENT Number 9

The Self Image can not tell the difference between what actually happens and what is vividly imagined.

Our imagination is extremely powerful. By rehearsing a 400 kneeling, my Self Image accepted as fact that it was like me to shoot a 400.

I use rehearsal to simulate training, when it is impossible to get to a range. While in the US Army, from 1976 to 1978, I was assigned to a non-shooting position at Ft. Sam Houston, Texas. I was 250 miles away from an international shooting range. During that two years, I was able to shoot on a range only six days.

I did not attend competitions, except the US nationals and team tryouts. Although I could not actually go to the range, I did continue training. I simulated shooting in my spare bedroom, a technique called dry firing, and I rehearsed daily. I made the USA team in 1978 and won the World Championships that year in Seoul, Korea.

Mental practice alone is no substitute for good range training, but it serves as an effective supplement, when actual training is not possible because of weather, injury or job assignment.

"Use Number 2– Controls Pressure"

What is Pressure? Pressure is the stress you experience when you are in competition, whether in business or sport. If you have to make a critical presentation, speak before a group or perform in the playoff, you have to deal with the pressure. Pressure can be divided into two parts 1) Anxiety and 2) Arousal.

Anxiety is fear. We fear many things. We fear serious injury. We fear the unknown. We fear the consequences of having a poor performance. We fear high places, closed in places, people and things we do not understand.

Fear is a Self Image attitude. It can be controlled. The first thing to remember is that fear is not always a bad thing. It is fear that keeps us from driving our automobile too fast. One of the best ways to control fear, is through experience. You will find that after you have been in the stressful situation often, the negative characteristics of fear will be reduced. Rehearsal can help by giving us mental experience. I competed in the Olympic Games twice physically, but thousands of times mentally. Rehearsal reduces fear.

The second part of pressure is arousal. Arousal is your level of excitement. If you are just awaking from a deep sleep, you are not aroused enough for your best performance. You are too relaxed. Also, if you have just been told that you have won 10 million dollars in the state lottery, you will be too aroused to perform well. There is a point in between relaxation and arousal where your mental performance is maximized. Arousal is like a bell shaped curve. On one side you are too excited and on the other too relaxed. In the center, between the two, is the optimum mental level, where your best performance can be achieved.

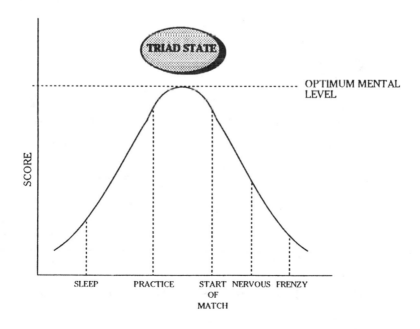

It is sometimes difficult to attain this optimum mental level. In training, you may be on the relaxed side of the arousal curve. Rehearsing that you are shooting well in a match, will move your arousal toward the optimum mental level. In competition, you may be on the excited side of the curve. Again, rehearsing that you are shooting exceptionally well, should relax you, moving you toward your optimum level.

Stress increases our level of excitement. If that level is too high or too low, you do not perform at your best. To reach the optimum mental level is your goal.

Rehearsing your desired performance, a few minutes before you begin, will help to center your concentration and move you toward your optimum mental level. I have seen world class high jumpers rehearse their exact steps, just before the jump. In fact, almost all world class athletes do some form of rehearsal before they perform. It is not uncommon to see top business executives using this tool to think through their next move to maximize their efficiency, in order to improve profitability.

"Use Number 3– Contingency Planning"

When NASA trains a space shuttle crew, more than half of the training, I am told, concerns what to do in case of contingencies.

In the Olympics, you must perform well Olympic day.

You do not get another chance for four years. There is the potential for tremendous pressure. In the 1976 Olympics, I was very calm. One of the reasons was because I had rehearsed over and over every possible thing that could happen in the match and my appropriate response.

Using Rehearsal to Improve Performance.

In 1976, during the final competitions leading up to the Olympics, I had the pleasure of working with Eva Funes, one of America's finest shotgun shooters. Eva's husband David related to me that she was unable to sleep the night before major competitions. If she lost her rest, she was unable to shoot well the next day. If she took sleeping pills, her reflexes were impaired. David asked if I knew of a mental management technique that would help her.

I told Eva that as long as she was going to be awake all night anyway, she might as well do something productive with her time. I told her to relax in bed and rehearse that she was shooting well in the match.

The next day, Eva Funes, rested from a good nights sleep, won the competition. When Eva began to rehearse shooting well, her level of arousal dropped, allowing her to sleep.

The Final Exam

Mary is taking her final exam tomorrow in college

algebra. She is frantic, knowing that a poor grade on the final will result in failure for the semester. Recalling a previous history of poor math finals in high school, Mary says, "I've no chance to pass that test!" With that attitude, Mary has little chance of passing her class.

Mary need not fail algebra. Mary should rehearse that she is in the classroom, taking the exam. The answers are coming easily to her. She passes the exam and the course. Rehearsal is no iron clad guarantee, but it can improve greatly your chances of success.

You may effectively use rehearsal to help you get through a negotiation, a law suit, surgery or an income tax audit.

Rehearsal is the most often used mental tool because it is logical, easy to use, convenient, inexpensive and most importantly, because it works.

CHAPTER EIGHT

Improving Concentration by Running a Mental Program

To become the best rifle shooter in the world, all I had to do was to learn two things.

Number 1: Perform well enough mentally and technically to score a ten.

Number 2: Repeat Number 1.

Winning requires a consistent mental picture. The best way I have found to achieve this kind of concentration is by utilizing a technique I call, "Running a Mental Program."

The mind is very much like a computer. If you input a series of thoughts, it is like running a program...A Mental Program. Most mental inconsistency occurs when the thought process varies from event to event. If you do not have the same conscious picture each time, you should not expect to duplicate the sub-conscious skill.

It is possible to duplicate the exact mental series of pictures, before every performance, thereby achieving mental consistency. I will explain this mental tool by using the tasks of shooting a ten, and making a golf shot, but it is easily applied to any activity.

A Mental Program accomplishes two critical functions.

1. The Mental Program is a series of thoughts, that, when pictured, will trigger the Sub-Conscious to perform the appropriate action.

2. The Mental Program controls the thought process, occupying the Conscious mind. An occupied Conscious mind cannot pressure out, choke or have a break in concentration.

The Mental Program should be "run" every time, for every shot. The program I use and teach has five steps or points. They are:

1. The Point of Initiation.

2. The Point of Attitude.

3. The Point of Direction.

4. The Point of Control.

5. The Point of Focus.

1. The Point of Initiation: This is the starting point of the program. In this case, the point of initiation is loading the rifle. Prior to loading, the shooter can think about almost anything as long as it is not negative. Counting your score before you are finished is always considered an error. The Point of Initiation may vary from person to person. Some may choose picking up the rifle as the starting point. Others may start the mental program after spotting the shot. It does not matter as long as it is consistent.

2. The Point of Attitude: Once the rifle is loaded, the shooter pictures what it <u>feels</u> like to get a ten. Picture the feeling of success. See the bullet hole in the center of the ten ring. How does it feel to perform at your best. As you picture this feeling, your Sub-Conscious moves you to get the ten.

3. The Point of Direction: Next, shift your concentration to what it <u>looks</u> like to get the ten. In this step, you rehearse getting a ten. You imagine proper sight alignment. You imagine the rifle fires. You have a proper follow through and ten is the result.

4. The Point of Control: In this step you center concentration on the most critical part of your action. In rifle shooting the point of control is to make the hold slow and small. Think slower...smaller...slower...smaller.

5. The Point of Focus: The point of focus is the last thing you picture before you fire the rifle and ends the mental program. My point of focus is centering the target in the front sight.

The following is a mental program for a golf shot.

1. Point of Initiation: Grip the club properly. You could also start with assuming the stance or even the club selection. It does not matter as long as it is consistent, shot to shot.

2. Point of Attitude: What does it feel like to hit the ball straight? Can you picture a long straight drive, right down the middle?

3. Point of Direction: Picture a smooth swing, solid contact with the ball, head in the proper position and good follow through.

4. Point of Control: Maintain balance and bring the club back straight.

5. Point of Focus: Focus on the ball, keeping the head down.

It is necessary to coordinate the mental activity of running the mental program with the physical activity of executing the shot. This takes some practice, but will come in time. Also, you should take care to run the program in training as well as in competition.

By running the mental program, you do not have time to think about anything negative. It is impossible to choke and run the program at the same time. You have to think about choking to choke. If you only run the program, there is no time to think about distractions. You do not have time to count your score. You cannot be distracted by other players. You are protected from failure. It is your insurance policy against a bad performance.

The Three Phases of a task.

Everything we do has three parts or phases. They are:

The Anticipation Phase...

The Action Phase...

The Reinforcement Phase...

The anticipation phase is what you think about immediately **before** you perform. Running a Mental Program is the anticipation phase of shooting a shot or hitting a golf ball. By running the Mental Program, you insure that each shot will be performed, exactly the same way.

The action phase is what you think about as you perform. When I shoot the shot, I think about follow through. I simply continue the hold, until the shot is well out of the barrel. The golfer also thinks about his follow through, as he hits the ball, to insure a good shot.

The reinforcement phase is what you think about immediately **after** you perform. If the shot has been successful, I say, "That's like me!" If the shot is not good I forget the shot and move directly to the anticipation phase of the next shot.

The difference between the champion and the average player lies in the edge the champion gains in the anticipation, action and reinforcement phases of performance. Champions carefully prepare for their tasks, concentrate properly while performing and reinforce all good results.

The Anticipation Phase

In 1972, as we were preparing to board the plane to journey to Munich, Germany for the Olympics, my team mate Jack Writer approached me with an idea. Both of us were taking two rifles to the games, a primary and a back-up. Jack suggested that I put his back-up rifle, in the gun box with my primary rifle, and he would do the same. The idea being, that if something happened to one box, we could both shoot in the Olympics. When we arrived at the range in Munich, my gun box was missing. It was recovered, in the locker of the Soviet weight lifting team, just one day before the competition began. Because of Writer's idea, I was able to train at the games, with my back-up rifle. Success is no accident. Proper attention to the anticipation phase can make the action more easily accomplished.

The Action Phase

In 1974, during the 1974 World Shooting Championships in Switzerland, I learned a valuable lesson concerning the action phase. I was a Texas boy, stationed in south Georgia. I had trained that year in temperatures between fifty and one hundred degrees. We had the final tryout and national championships at Phoenix, Arizona in June. I won the tryout in temperatures of over one hundred degrees.

When the competition began, snow was falling. The temperature was four degrees and I was COLD. I had never shot in snow in my life. I was shooting the three hundred meter event. The snow was falling so hard, that I could not see the target at all. I was certain that they would postpone the match.

"Commence Firing!" The match started. I could not see the target. I was frustrated. Just then I heard the shooter next to me shoot. I couldn't believe it. What was he shooting at? As I looked down range I saw that, for an instant, the snow parted and the targets could be seen. The Swiss shooters are experienced in shooting under these conditions. I had no time, nor the opportunity, to become an experienced snow shooter. If I were going to win, I had to shoot as if I had lived in the mountains all my life. I said to myself, "I am the best snow shooter on this range! I shoot in the snow all the time! I love shooting in the snow!" I watched the Swiss shooter next to me. Every time he readied to shoot, I would follow his lead. I won the match.

Sometimes when your best is not good enough, you have to do whatever is required.

The Reinforcement Phase

I have discovered, in my twelve years as a teacher, that most world class athletes do well in the anticipation and action phases. A breakdown often occurs in the reinforcement phase. I see far too many athletes reinforcing their bad performances by thinking and talking about them. Every time you talk about a bad performance, you improve the probability, of having another one, just like it, in the future.

I was very fortunate. The years I competed for the United States, the best shooters in the world were Americans. I knew, to win, I had to defeat my team mates.

Jack Writer (World and Olympic Champion), Lones Wigger (World and Olympic Champion) and Margaret Murdock (World and Olympic Silver medalist) were vicious competitors. One thing, I especially remember about training with them, was that they never talked about their failures in front of me. If Wigger had a problem, he kept it to himself. I asked him about that once. He said he didn't want to give any of us an edge, thinking he was having a challenge. He once told me, "Bassham, you will likely beat me four out of five times that we shoot against each other, but I plan to make my one time count." He was the toughest shooter, in big competitions, I ever faced.

Jack Writer was a talker. It was not that Jack bragged on himself, although I can understand, how those who didn't know him would think that. Jack just liked to talk. His favorite subject was shooting and he was his favorite shooter. No matter how many low scores he shot, Jack would only talk about the high ones. The important lesson here, is that Writer never reinforced a bad performance and rarely shot a low score in a big match. If I had to select only one shooter as my partner in a two-man team match, it would be Jack Writer.

Margaret Murdoch rarely talked at all. If she did, it was normally to complement others on their performance. I wonder if she knew, that every time she praised another shooter, she improved her chances of winning?

All three of these champions excelled in the reinforcement phase, each in their own, unique manner.

How well prepared are you for your task? Are you performing below your potential because you are not properly prepared?

How well do you perform when the circumstances are different from those you have anticipated?

What do you reinforce? Do you praise others when they perform well? Do you praise yourself?

Part III

"Building the Sub-Conscious Circle"

CHAPTER NINE

"The Skills Factory"

I don't think I have a natural ability for shooting. In fact, I am still searching for my a special talent. I have known athletes that seem to have a gift for their sport. One such shooter is Soma Dutta from India.

I met Soma, for the first time, in 1982. Her family, eager to find an international shooting coach, accompanied her to Seguin, to check me out. Soma stayed at the International Shooting School for one month as we evaluated each other. At the young age of 14, this resident of Calcutta, held every major national record in her country. Her women and junior records exceeded the best results recorded by the men as well.

Gifted, is the only word I know to explain this incredible young athlete. Just as a great artist seems to see the paintings in the mind before they are translated to canvas, Soma had a special "feel" for her positions. Most shooters tire of training after four to five hours. If I would allow it, she would spend ten. I would make her take a day off and find her sneaking up to the range to shoot.

Soma returned to the school the next year for two months. She shot in the Olympic in 1984 at sixteen, the youngest shooter on the line. For the past four years, she has been a full time resident student at the International Shooting School. She is ranked second in Asia and among the top twenty in the world. She won the coveted quota slot, awarded to less than forty shooters in the world, qualifying her to compete in the 1988 Olympic Games in Seoul.

The advantage the gifted athlete possesses is difficult to measure. Obviously, it is not necessary to be especially talented to win the Olympics. I am proof of that. Certain things come easier to the talented ones, for the rest of us, hard work is the great equalizer. Although it is difficult to compare myself to Soma, I feel secure in saying that, she masters shooting techniques three to five times faster, than I did. The big advantage to talent is that it saves time. If you are not particularly talented, take heart, it may take you a little longer, but, you can catch and surpass a talented athlete, if you train effectively.

Your skills are developed in the Sub-Conscious mind. The amount of skill and the size of the Sub-Conscious circle is determined by several factors. They are 1) How often you train, 2) How efficiently you train, and 3) What you reinforce. To best understand training we will look at the seven guidelines to building Sub-Conscious skills.

Training Guideline Number 1.

"Catch Yourself Doing Something Right!"

I hear, all too often, the comment, "What am I doing wrong?" If I could only isolate my problem areas and find the cause of my failures, I could be a success. Nothing could be further from the truth. That is like saying, "If I study all the wrong ways of doing a math problem, I will learn better how to do it right!" What you really need to do is study only one way of doing things, THE RIGHT WAY!. Isn't it so much easier to study only one way to do something right than one hundred ways to do it wrong? If you study failure, you will become an expert in HOW TO FAIL!

Therefore, stop catching yourself doing things wrong and trying to find out why you are failing. Instead, only think about your successes, never your failures. An example is the golfer. The mentally uninformed golfer hits a good shot and says, "Well, I guess I just got lucky that time!" When he hits a bad shot he says, "Why do I always do that?" The mentally informed golfer hits a bad shot. He knows it is bad but says, "Next time I will hit a better shot!" Then he hits a good shot and says, "That's a good shot. What did I do right?" See the difference?

Training Guideline Number 2.

"Train Four or Five Days a Week."

You cannot become better at your skill if you do not train regularly. However, the best athletes in the world do not train seven days a week. How much is too much and how much is not enough? For most activities, business and sport, you will burn out if you do them seven days a week. And if you do less than four, you will not maximize your chance to improve.

If you train only one day a week, it is probable that you will deteriorate faster than if you do not train at all. That's right, one day a week is worse than no training at all. If you train two or three days a week, you can maintain your level, but you may not improve. Therefore, train four or five days a week, to maximize your performance.

Training Guideline Number 3.

"Where ever you are...Be all there!"

When you go from the office to the tennis court, leave the office thoughts in the office. When you go home to the family, leave the bad tennis loss on the court. When you go the the office from home, leave the problems of home at home! Where ever you are, be there 100%.

Training Guideline Number 4.

"Rehearse the Match Day, Within the Training Session."

Treat every training day as if it had the same importance as the most critical competition day. You can do that by rehearsing in your mind, that this IS the competition. Try to imagine in every practice session that it is the match. See it, hear it, taste it, smell it, and feel the match. Make your rehearsal vivid.

Training Guideline Number 5.

"When You are Shooting Good....Shoot a Lot!"

This is an expression I borrowed from my team mate in the Olympics, John Writer. I am sure it applies to your field of interest as well. I remember one day Jack and I were training together. I asked him what he was going to shoot that day.

"I will shoot fifty shots in the standing position and one hundred shots in kneeling."

"I will do the same thing."

We both started shooting standing. Soon I finished my fifty shots and started kneeling. Jack continued in standing. After I finished my one hundred shots kneeling, Jack was still in standing. I went to lunch. When I returned, Jack was still shooting standing. Finally, he finished. I asked him why he changed his mind and shot so much standing. That's when he told me, "I was shooting above my record. When I do that I always keep shooting. You see, when you are shooting good, shoot a lot!" Likewise, if you are having a bad day, STOP TRAINING. Do no practice losing!

CHAPTER TEN

Performance Analysis

We know from the Mental Management Principle of Reinforcement that we should write down everything that we do correctly. How is this done?

For many years I fought the concept of keeping a performance journal or diary. I worked hard in training and I wanted to eliminate any superfluous activities. It was not until I discovered a journal keeping system, that I knew I couldn't live without a journal. Training and match scores improved and were much more consistent. I was able to review my progress and better evaluate my efforts using a systematic approach to record keeping. The system I use is called Performance Analysis.

Performance analysis is the process of recording in your performance journal essential information, tracking your progress. It is a complete system, taking only a few minutes a day, that utilizes positive reinforcement to speed you toward your goal.

Why use a performance journal? A plan is not easily followed, if it is not written down. It is of no use, if you cannot readily refer to it.

A journal keeps a written record of six key planning areas.

1. Your schedule.

2. Your diary.

3. Your solution analysis.

4. Your success analysis.

5. Your daily goal statement.

6. Your index of often used addresses and phone numbers.

Your journal should be in a binder that allows you to add and remove pages. It should be carried with you to all training sessions. There is a page for each day, with sufficient space to enter the needed data. The purpose of the journal is to add organization to your training program, not burden you with unnecessary work.

Now let's look at each part of the journal page.

(1) Your schedule identifies time slots that you plan to devote to some area of your training. If you do not train that day or do anything that affects your sport or activity, such as ordering equipment, you will not fill out a journal page for that day. Fill out the data section of the schedule.

The data section contains the date, location, event (training or competition) and the time of day and time period of the activity.

(2) The next section is called the diary. Simply write down exactly what you accomplished during this period. How many shots did you shoot? How many hours did you train? How did you spend the time? You cannot lie to a journal.

Three ladies are at a swimming pool. One sits in the sun, never entering the water. One puts her feet in the water but does not leave the pool side. One swims 20 laps of the pool. Later, when asked, all three will say they had been swimming that day. It is easy for us to say we are training, when in fact we are spending most of our time visiting with other competitors, setting up equipment, or reflecting upon our condition, whatever it may be.

A journal diary entry eliminates rationalizations and records the facts.

(3) Solution analysis is your chance to write down any solutions to challenges that you have discovered today. If you have a problem that you can not find a solution for, simply state, "I'm looking for a solution to ...stating the problem." Also you should write down anything newly learned today, in this section.

(4) In the success analysis section, write down anything you did well today. You have just improved the

probability that you will repeat the success. If you have recorded a personal record, this section should be quite descriptive on this day. The journal forces you to be positive about your sport.

(5) The goal statement is the most important step of the journal page. State an objective that you intend to reach in the first person present tense, as if you have already reached it. Some examples of goal statements are:

"I often shoot above 390/400."

"I am on the United States Olympic development team."

"I always sell at least four contracts a week."

"I shoot par golf."

"I am the most valuable player on our team."

Goal statements should be goals that are out of reach, but not out of sight. Every time we write down a goal we are that much closer to its attainment. Only two things are possible. Your goal will be reached or you will stop writing it down. As long as you continue to write down your goal statements, you are moving toward their attainment.

(6) Keep these addresses and phone numbers in your address pages:

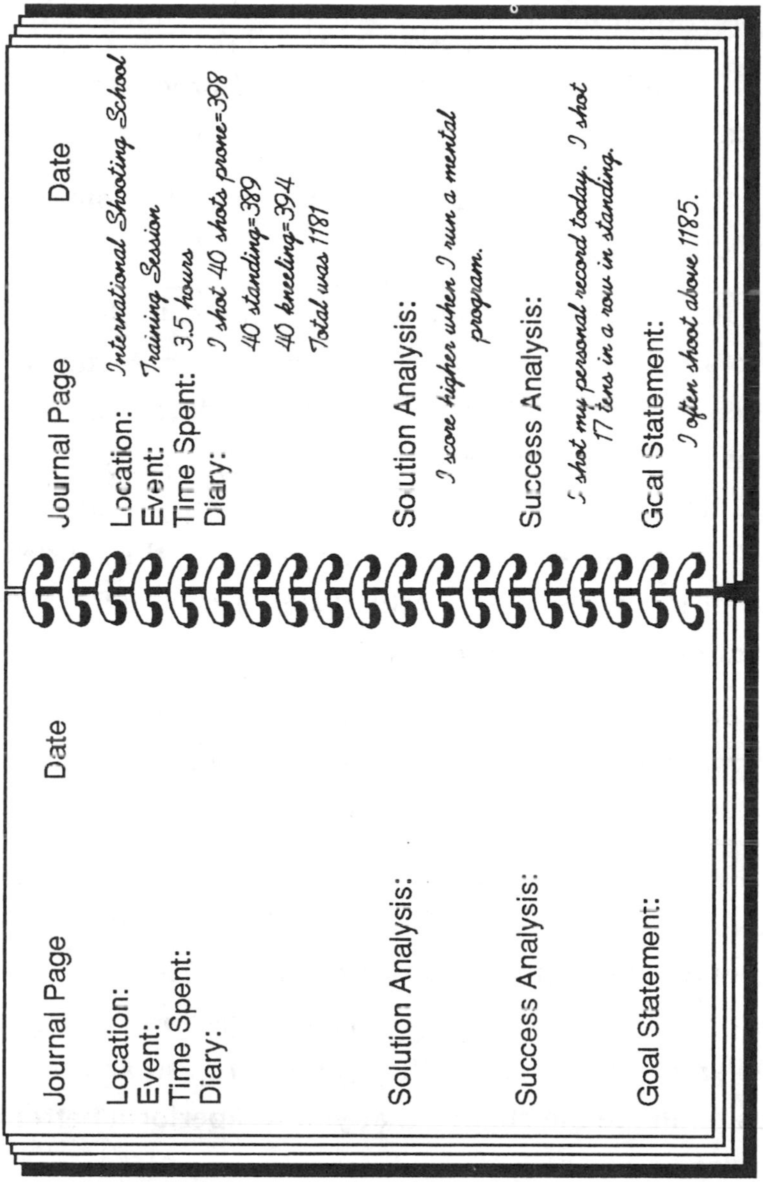

Journal Page   Date

Location:
Event:
Time Spent:
Diary:

Solution Analysis:

Success Analysis:

Goal Statement:

Journal Page   Date

Location: *International Shooting School*
Event: *Training Session*
Time Spent: *3.5 hours*
Diary: *I shot 40 shots prone=398*
         40 standing=389
         40 kneeling=394
         Total was 1181

Solution Analysis:
     I score higher when I run a mental program.

Success Analysis:
     I shot my personal record today. I shot 17 tens in a row in standing.

Goal Statement:
     I often shoot above 1185.

Figure 10.0

A. Participants in your sport, coaches, administrators, organizers.

B. Manufacturers and marketers of products you use in your sport.

C. Hotels, motels and restaurants near the competitions, you frequent.

Performance analysis is one of the most useful coaching tools available. I can learn much from a review of a students journals. I discover how many days a week the student is training. I know how many hours a day is spent in practice and exactly what was accomplished. I am immediately aware of the problem areas of the students and their strengths. I know the goals of my students and most importantly, they do as well.

A performance journal provides the athlete and coach with a valuable resource for improvement, without burdening either with unnecessary paperwork.

Be careful to safeguard your journal. I lost my Olympic journal sometime in late 1976. I recommend that you remove the journal pages monthly, storing them in a safe place. Continued reference to your performance analysis will reduce the chance that you will repeat an error as well as reinforce the chance that you will perform better in the future.

Guidelines for Building a Training Program

Another use for the journal is to aid in documenting your training program. I will use shooting as the example, but again, the guidelines are easily translated to any sport.

1. You should begin by determining the competition schedule for the year. In most sports, there are several big meets scheduled for the year, culminating in the Nationals. Schedule these events on your master calendar, in the space provided in your journal.

2. Next, you should count the number of training days, you have available to you, from the present to the next competition. Now, count the days available for the entire year. You may be surprised just how few there are.

Look for possible conflicts to your being able to attend these critical events. College students may not be able to move their finals to go to a match, but they might be able to register for classes that allow them to have Fridays free as a travel day. Try to maximize the hours you have available by planning in advance. Too many times, valuable training is lost because we run out of supplies, such as targets or ammunition.

3. Next, you should file a training budget. If you are fortunate, you have a coach or manager that can help you with this step. A training budget has projections for at least four areas. Equipment, Travel, Fees and Supplies.

A. Equipment. What new equipment will you need to reach your goals for the year? What is your plan to acquire them and when is the best time to make the purchase?

B. What are the travel costs to get to matches, seminars or training sessions? By planning in advance, you may be able to save on advance purchase for air fare or combine two competitions into one trip.

C. Fees are the expenses charged for entering competitions, national association memberships, seminar and coaching expenses.

D. The supplies you use include ammunition, targets and cleaning supplies. Avoid the possibility of lost training days by scheduling advanced purchases of these critical items.

4. You divide your year into quarter sessions. The length of the quarters are individual and sport specific. These are:

First Quarter: Evaluation.

You have just finished a needed rest from last season's competitions. During this session, you should establish your training plan, make out your budget and set your schedule for the year. You should evaluate any equipment or technique changes you plan to make in the coming competitive year. Now is the time to try that new idea that you had during your reflection session. Order the new equipment, test it out and make improvements during this session. Later in the competition quarter, you will not want to be changing things in the middle of the season.

Second Quarter: Conditioning.

In this quarter, you work especially hard on drills that will strengthen you for the demanding season ahead. Shooting is not a seasonal sport. We shoot major competitions year round. If your sport is not seasonal, you may have to compete within the conditioning session. If so, understand that your competition has the same challenge. It was always motivating to me to shoot against my major competitors in the winter season. If I seemed behind, I worked harder. If I was ahead, I worked even harder because I knew that the competition would be trying to catch me.

Third Quarter: Competition.

During this period, you will be attending major competitions leading up to your national championship. By this time, you should be properly conditioned and at your best. The focus in this session is peak performance. Training centers on match simulations rather than drills.

Experimentation with new equipment and technique is avoided.

Fourth Quarter: Rest and Reflection.

The season is over. You have done your best in the nationals. It is a time for much needed rest, repair and reflection. Do not make the mistake of omitting this step. You may think that you can get a jump on your competition by training at this time, but chances are, that you will weaken yourself in the long run. Also, you need the time away from your sport to reflect on your goals, training methods and concepts. It is during this period, that you establish an outline for your training during the year.

5. Next, you should set up training objectives for the year in three major areas. First, determine how many hours you will average in each training day. Second, select an overall plan as to how you will spend those hours. Thirdly, determine what objectives you want to be meeting in training, by the end of each quarter session?

By following these guidelines, you should develop a well planned training program that should improve your results in competition.

Part IV

"Building the Self Image Circle"

(HABITS)
SELF IMAGE
(ATTITUDES)

CHAPTER ELEVEN

"Building a Better You."

The Self Image is the sum of your habits and attitudes. Your attitudes determine whether you feel positively or negatively about an item or concept. Your habits determine how you act. You will do certain things because it is consistent with your Self Image.

Are these attitudes familiar?

"I perform great in practice, but when I get in the match my score drops."

"If I do well at the beginning, I loose it at the end."

"I seem to always be so busy, but I just don't seem to get much done."

"I can never remember names."

"I can't sell anything, I'm not that kind of person."

"I could never speak before a large crowd of people."

"I'm technically sound in my sport, but I choke under pressure."

These are statements I've heard from students of mine. They are all temporary Self Image attitudes. They can change.

In fact, the same people that held these attitudes initially, soon began to talk like this.

"I perform better in matches than in practice."

"If I start well, I finish well."

"I am an efficient person that gets things done."

"I'm good at remembering names."

"I enjoy speaking before groups."

"I'm the kind of person that people order from."

"I can count on a good performance, especially under pressure."

What accounted for the change? They all experienced a change in Self Image. When you shift the Self Image, the change is permanent.

We tend to perform within a certain "comfort zone". I bowl between 120 and 160. It is not like me to bowl below 120 or above 160. It is like me to bowl an occasional strike, but I have never bowled four in a row. "It is not like me!" I get nervous if I ever get three in a row. My comfort zone is set between 120 and 160. That's like me.

Your Self Image "makes you act like you!" It keeps you within your comfort zone. If you are below your zone, your Self Image makes you uncomfortable and turns up your power until you within the zone. Likewise, if you are above your zone, the Self Image will cut your power, dropping you back within your zone. As long as you "act like you" the Self Image is content and does not interfere. To change your performance you must change your Self Image and MOVE YOUR ZONE.

For ambitious people, changing their own Self Image is the most important skill they will ever learn. You can change any attitude that is keeping you from your goal. When the Self Image changes, performance changes.

To change Self Image one must accomplish four very important tasks.

1. You must be willing to undergo change.

2. You must identify the habits and attitudes that you need to change.

3. You must set up a new Self Image that is in direct conflict with your old self.

4. You must exchange your old Self Image for the new Self Image.

Task Number 1: *You must be willing to change.*

Nothing is going to change, unless you change. If you possessed all that you needed to succeed, you would have reached your goal already.

As an example, Donny was a fine young basketball

player who had a chance to make his schools starting squad. His defensive ability was solid. He was a good shooter, but his percentage at the free throw line was poor. So poor in fact, that the coach hesitated to play him in critical situations. The coach knew, that Donny's deficiency was a mental attitude about the free throw line. When questioned about his not starting, Donny would say, "The coach just likes the other player better. I just don't shoot free throws well, I never have." With that attitude Donny had no chance to start. Also Donny has a bad habit of getting mad when he misses a free throw, thereby reinforcing his error. Donny needed to change his Self Image. His attitude needed to be "I am the best free throw shooter on the team."

One day Donny approached the coach.

"OK coach, I'm ready to do whatever it takes to make the starting squad. What do I have to do?"

"Are you ready to change your attitude about making free throws?

"Yes sir, I'm ready!"

Task **number** **2:** *Identify the attitudes and habits you need to change.*

How do we identify which habits and attitudes we need to change? It is easier than you think. Simply look at the problems you are having and start there. If you turn your weaknesses into strengths your performance will surely benefit. In this regard, problems and frustrations are valuable keys to our success. For skilled athletes and business professionals, most of the time, their problems are with negative attitudes and poor reinforcement.

In our example, Donny needs to change one attitude and one habit. The attitude that needs changing is that of "I am not a good free throw shooter." The habit that must be eliminated is that of reinforcing his missed shots.

<u>Task</u> <u>Number</u> <u>3:</u> *Set up a new Self Image that is in direct conflict with your old habits and attitudes.*

Donny's new attitude is "I am the best free throw shooter on my team." His new habit is, that each time he makes a free throw he must say, "That's like me!" Each time he misses he must forget his error. Olympic athletes call this technique "Feast or Forget."

He must run a mental program on each free throw, to maximize his chance of making every shot. He should reinforce his successes by recording his performance analysis in his journal.

<u>Task</u> <u>Number</u> <u>4:</u> *Change your Self Image.*

Replacing an old Self Image with a new one is no simple matter. Our habits and attitudes were instilled over a long period of time, and are not easily dislodged. Care must be taken in attempting any process that can so alter ones behavior. The mental process that I endorse is both safe and extremely effective. It has been carefully evaluated by the coaches and professional staffs of the Olympic teams of a half a dozen nations. It is called the Directive Affirmation.

CHAPTER TWELVE

"The Most Powerful Tool in Mental Management-
The Directive Affirmation."

Developed, in its present form, shortly before the Olympics in 1976, I personally credit this tool, as having the greatest single effect on my success in athletics and business, of any mental concept I have used. I call the process the Directive Affirmation.

Once you have mastered this Mental Management tool, you can change anything you do not like about yourself. You can use the Directive Affirmation, to help you achieve anything you desire in your life. This concept is not magic, but it certainly seems to work like it. I have personally used this tool, to help win the 1976 Olympics and the World Championships in 1978.

The Directive Affirmation is effective in increasing productivity, reducing the negative effects of stress and creating winning attitudes.

Simply put, the Directive Affirmation is a paragraph in the first person present tense that describes a persons goal, pay value, plan, habits and attitudes, that is rehearsed repetitively causing the Self Image to change.

To illustrate how the tool works, we will use the example of our basketball player, Donny.

Steps in writing a Directive Affirmation:

Step 1. Define the goal...To become the best free throw shooter on my team.

Step 2. Set the time limit...By 1st November next year.

Step 3. List the personal pay value of reaching this goal...I will be a starter on the basketball team. I will aid in my teams effort to win because I score well at the free throw line.

Step 4. Outline the plan to achieve the goal.

A. Run a Mental Program before each free throw in practice and in games.

B. Every time I score I will say "That's like me!"

C. Record my performance analysis daily.

D. Read and visualize my Directive Affirmations daily.

Step 5. Write a Directive Affirmation in the first person present tense, beginning with the word I. State the goal as if you already are in possession of it. Next list the pay value. List your plan to reach your goal. Restate the goal. Date the paragraph with your target date.

11/1/89

"I am the best free throw shooter on my team. I start each game and enjoy the chance to help my team win by making free throws. I always run a mental program before each shot, reinforce each basket by saying "That's Like Me!", record my performance analysis and read and visualize my Directive Affirmation daily. I am the best free throw shooter on my team."

Step 6: Make 5 copies of the Directive Affirmation in your own hand writing on index file cards.

Step 7: Place the cards in five prominent places, ie..on your bathroom mirror, on the refrigerator door, on your desk, on your computer terminal, on the bedroom door, as a book mark in the book you are reading.

Step 8: Read and visualize your Directive Affirmation each time you come to a key point. See yourself as the person in the Directive Affirmation. Soon you will become this person as your Self Image changes and your performance will sub-consciously improve.

A key point is a suitable location for a Directive Affirmation card. It should be a place that you visit often in your normal day. Donny has chosen as his five key points, the refrigerator door, the bathroom mirror, the door to his bedroom, his desk in his room and the lamp by his bed. Each time Donny comes to a key point, he must read and visualize the Directive Affirmation.

When Donny begins to read the Directive Affirmation, he sees himself as being the best free throw shooter of his team. He pictures starting every game and making a contribution to his team. He sees himself running a mental program, sinking the basket and saying "That's Like Me!" Donny records his successes in his performance journal and reads and visualizes his Directive Affirmations daily. Each session should only take a few minutes.

This is not the way Donny has thought in the past. This new Self Image is in direct conflict with his old Self Image. The Self Image cannot stand a conflict. Something has to go... The new Self Image or the old one. As Donny continues to visualize the "new Donny" in the Directive Affirmation, at some point, the conflict is resolved by the exchange of the old attitudes and habits with the new ones. Wham! The Self Image is changed and Donny starts sinking free throws.

Reshaping the mind is much like reshaping the physical body. If you are overweight, it is likely that the cause is repetitive over eating. Repetitive change of your eating habits is the best way to bring your weight down safely. If you have a poor attitude, it is likely that the cause is repetitive negative reinforcement. Repetitive change of your thinking habits is the best way to bring about an attitude change.

The real power in the Directive Affirmation is that it requires the user to:

1. Set a goal.

2. List a pay value.

3. Set a time limit.

4. Identify a plan to get the goal by changing an attitude or habit of both.

5. Repeat over & over each day a positive picture.

Does this sound familiar? You know that you should do these things, but unless there is a way to require you to do them, you won't! How many times have you read a self improvement book or attended a seminar, after which you came home all excited, but two weeks later you were the same old person. If any change occurred in you at all, it was temporary.

The Directive Affirmation is a tool to affect <u>permanent change</u>. If you follow the steps in the Directive Affirmation carefully, there are only two possible outcomes. Either you will become the person you want to be or you will stop reading the affirmation. It is that simple.

CHAPTER THIRTEEN

"Making the Directive Affirmation Work for You!"

In my more than fifteen years experience using and teaching the Directive Affirmation, I have seen results in a broad range of applications. In this chapter I will list several examples of Directive Affirmations as applied to a variety of success areas.

Directive Affirmation Example #1.

Weight Control

I feel that the major reason that people are not successful in dieting is that they have their goal stated incorrectly. If you are ten pounds overweight, the goal should not be to lose ten pounds.

If your goal is to lose weight, this may happen.

Step 1. You go on your favorite diet. This normally means that you must alter your eating habits. This is not like you and your old Self Image begins to fight you from the very beginning.

Step 2. You persist and after some time you notice a drop of a few pounds. Since your goal is to lose ten pounds, you continue until you are ten pounds lighter.

Step 3. Then an amazing thing happens. In order for you to continue to reach your goal of losing weight, you must gain weight again. Soon you are ten pounds heavy again. The cycle goes on and on. I know people that have lost one thousand pounds with this method, ten pounds at a time.

A better way is to set the correct goal. If you weigh 170 and want to weigh 160, then set the goal to maintain a fit 160 pound weight.

Let's set up a Directive Affirmation to achieve a desired body weight. Using the Directive Affirmation, you will not only find that your diet is more easily followed, but you will also notice a change in Self Image. You will not have to lose the weight again.

The Directive Affirmation:

Step 1. Define the goal...To weigh 160 pounds.

Step 2. Set the time limit...By 1 November next year.

Step 3. List the personal pay value of reaching this-goal...I feel better and look better at 160. I can wear my best suit comfortably.

Step 4. Outline the plan to achieve the goal.

A. Eat fruit for breakfast.

B. Drink a food supplement or eat a food bar for lunch.

C. Eat only at mealtimes (no snacks between meals).

D. Ride exercise bike daily for 30 minutes.

E. Read and visualize my Directive Affirmations daily.

Step 5. Write a Directive Affirmation.

11/1/89

"I weigh 160 pounds. I feel and look great at 160. I enjoy wearing my best suit in comfort. I eat fruit for breakfast, food bar or liquid supplement for lunch and only eat at mealtimes. I ride my exercise bike daily for 30 minutes. I read and visualize my Directive Affirmations daily. I weigh 160 pounds."

Directive Affirmation Example# 2.

The Non-Smoker

Many smokers find it difficult to stop smoking and not return to their old Self Image of being a smoker. Again, I feel the difficulty is due to setting the wrong goal. The goal should not be to stop smoking, it should be to become a non-smoker. If your goal is to stop smoking, in order to continue to attain your goal, it is necessary to begin again. You stop, then start, then stop, then start again. There is a better way. With the Directive Affirmation, there is permanent change.

The Directive Affirmation:

Step 1. Define the goal...To become a non-smoker.

Step 2. Set the time limit...By 1st November next year.

Step 3. List the personal pay value of reaching this goal...I have prolonged endurance, more energy and longer life expectancy.

Step 4. Outline the plan to achieve the goal.

  A. I permit no cigarettes in my home.

  B. I chew gum when I feel like smoking.

  C. I say continually, "I control my life."

  D. Read and visualize my Directive Affirmations daily.

Step 5. Write a Directive Affirmation.

11/1/89

"I enjoy being a Non-Smoker. I feel strong, healthy, with more energy and I know I will live longer. I permit no cigarettes in my home. I chew gum when needed and I continually say 'I control my life, not a chemical.' I read and visualize my Directive Affirmations daily. I enjoy being a Non-Smoker."

Directive Affirmation Example # 3.

Making an Olympic Shooting Team

I thought you might like to see the Directive Affirmation I utilized to make the USA Olympic team in 1976. The same format can be used for any high level goal for competition.

The Directive Affirmation:

Step 1. Define the goal... To become a member of the 1976 US Olympic Shooting Team.

Step 2. Set the time limit... By 1 July 1976.

Step 3. List the personal pay value of reaching this goal...

A. I have taken my next step toward winning the Olympic Games.

B. I enjoy the recognition of being one of the best shooters in my country.

C. I have qualified for an all expense paid trip to Montreal Canada to compete for the Olympic Gold Medal.

Step 4. Outline the plan to achieve the goal.

A. Use ultimate you actual rehearsal before each stage, run a mental program on each shot, record my performance analysis daily and

99

rehearse winning the Gold medal each evening.

C. Train six days a week, five hours a day using progressive training of dry firing, group shooting and live shooting.

D. Jog three miles, four times a week.

E. Supplement my diet with Nutrilite XX daily.

F. Read and visualize my Directive Affirmations daily.

Step 5. Write a Directive Affirmation.

7/1/76

"I am a member of the 1976 US Olympic Shooting Team. I have taken my next step toward the accomplishment of my lifelong goal of an Olympic Gold medal. I enjoy the recognition as one of the best shooters in my country. I look forward to the all expense paid trip to Montreal to compete at the games. I always use ultimate you actual rehearsal before each shooting session, run a mental program on each shot, record my performance analysis daily and rehearse winning the Gold medal each evening. I train six days a week, five hours a day, utilizing progressive training, dry firing, group shooting and live shooting. I jog three miles, four times a week and eat my Nutrilite XX food supplement daily. I read and visualize my Directive Affirmations daily. I am a member of the 1976 US Olympic Shooting Team."

Directive Affirmation Example # 4.

Remembering Names

Occasionally, we need an affirmation to change something about ourselves that we do not like. Some of us are poor at remembering names. This Directive Affirmation should make you good at remembering names, for the rest of your life.

The Directive Affirmation:

Step 1. Define the goal...To become good at remembering names.

Step 2. Set the time limit...Thirty days from todays date.

Step 3. List the personal pay value of reaching this goal...

  A. I feel good when I can remember a persons name.

  B. They feel good as well.

  C. Remembering names is good for business.

Step 4. Outline the plan to achieve the goal.

The major reason why people cannot remember the names of others is that they have poor name remembering habits. When most of us meet a new person, we do not even hear their name. We are too busy saying our own name. If you will implement the following habits, you will become gifted in recalling names.

When I meet a new person I:

A. Repeat their name.

B. Spell it.

C. Form an association with their name and a familiar item.

D. Later write it down.

Step 5. Write a Directive Affirmation.

6/1/88

"I am good at remembering names. When I recall a new persons name, it makes me feel good, them feel good and it is good for business. When I meet a new person, I always repeat their name, spell it, form an association and later write it down. I am good at remembering names."

Directive Affirmation Example # 5.

The Time Manager

Time is the only asset that you cannot recover once it is lost. Becoming a good time manager should be high on any successful persons list of skills. There are many useful books available on time management. Many people find implementing the suggestions in these books difficult. The Directive Affirmation is just the tool to solve this difficulty.

The Directive Affirmation:

Step 1. Define the goal...To become a good time manager.

Step 2. Set the time limit...Within sixty days of todays date.

Step 3. List the personal pay value of reaching this goal...

  A. I feel organized.

  B. I get many things done in a short time.

  C. I can find the information I am looking for easily.

Step 4. Outline the plan to achieve the goal.

  A. I keep all my notes, calender, addresses, and schedules in a journal that I keep with me always.

  B. I write out a things to do list before the beginning of each day, ranking each item and scheduling the most important first.

  C. I keep a clear desk and work on only one item at a time.

Step 5. Write a Directive Affirmation.

8/1/88

"I am a good manager of my time. I am well organized, getting things done in an efficient, timely manner. I can find information that I am looking for easily. I keep all my notes, calender, addresses, and schedules in a journal that I keep with me always. I write out a things to do list before the beginning of each day, ranking each item and scheduling the most important first. I keep a clear desk and work on only one item at a time. I am a good manager of my time."

Directive Affirmation Example # 6.

<u>Debt</u> <u>Free</u>

Yes, one can even use the Directive Affirmation to help with the bills. It seems that we live in a day of credit cards and easy money. With the inflating costs of homes and autos, it is no wonder that most people must deal with debt more and more.

I feel that the major reason that more people are not debt free is that they never goal set to become debt free. We often goal set to increase our income, but when the income increases, we simply increase our "needs." The Directive Affirmation can help.

The Directive Affirmation:

Step 1. Define the goal...To become debt free. To owe no one.

Step 2. Set the time limit...Within fifteen years of todays date.

Step 3. List the personal pay value of reaching this goal...

Debt equals stress. Imagine life with no mortgage, no credit card balances, no loans outstanding and no fear of bankruptcy.

Step 4. Outline the plan to achieve the goal.

A. Invest ten percent of all you earn in an interest bearing program.

B. Stop all card and credit purchases.

C. Set up a budget to live on less than you earn, applying the difference toward reducing the debt.

D. Aggressively seek out opportunity to increase your income, applying the increase toward the debt.

Step 5. Write a Directive Affirmation.

12/1/88

"I am debt free. I pay no interest. I have no mortgage, no credit card balances and no loans due. I am
financially free. I invest ten percent of everything I
earn in an interest bearing program. I stopped all
card card and credit purchases. I set up a budget to
live on less than I earn, applying the difference
toward reducing debt. I aggressively seek out opportunity to increase my income, applying a portion of
the increase toward the debt. I am debt free."

Directive Affirmation Example # 7.

Passing the Exam

For those of you that are students, concerned about
finals or professionals, concerned about state boards, this
is the Directive Affirmation that will work for you.

The Directive Affirmation:

Step 1. Define the goal...To make an "A" on the final
exam in Mental Management 101.

Step 2. Set the time limit...exam date.

Step 3. List the personal pay value of reaching this
goal...

A. Passing the exam is necessary for passing the
course.
B. I will have taken a vital step toward graduation.

C. I will enjoy the feeling of scoring high on the exam.

Step 4. Outline the plan to achieve the goal.

A. I prepare for the classes by reading the assigned text before class and finishing the homework.

B. I take good notes daily in class

C. I study adequately for the final.

D. I rehearse taking the final, knowing the answers and scoring well.

E. Read and visualize my Directive Affirmation daily.

Step 5. Write a Directive Affirmation.

12/1/89

"I made an 'A' on my final exam in Mental Management 101. I enjoy the feeling of making a top grade on this final. I have passed the course and taken a vital step toward graduation from the Thrill of Victory University. I prepared for the final by reading the assigned text, turning in my homework in a timely manner, taking good notes and studying for the exams. I rehearsed taking the final, knowing the answers and scoring well. I read and visualize my Directive Affirmation daily. I made an 'A' on my final exam in Mental Management 101."

Directive Affirmation Example # 8.

A Better Job

A Directive Affirmation can be written for any goal, even if you are unsure of a plan to acquire the goal. Here is an example a student of mine used to facilitate a job change.

The Directive Affirmation:

Step 1. Define the goal...To acquire a new job with a higher salary than I presently earn, without having to move from the city.

Step 2. Set the time limit...six months from today's date.

Step 3. List the personal pay value of reaching this goal...

  A. More money to improve my life style.

  B. Change in job will eliminate burn out.

  C. I will enjoy the feeling of moving upward in my community.

Step 4. Outline the plan to achieve the goal.

  A. Looking for a way to obtain a better paying position.

  B. Rehearsing I am offered a new job with higher pay.

C. Read and visualize my Directive Affirmation daily.

Step 5. Write a Directive Affirmation.

12/1/89

"I enjoy my new job here in my community. I enjoy the feeling of moving up in my financial position. I am excited about the increased income I am receiving. I found this new job by staying open to any new idea that would increase my income, rehearsing that I was offered a higher paying position in the city and reading an visualizing my Directive Affirmation Daily."

Write a Directive Affirmation for your goal, using the examples in this chapter. Make sure you follow the checks below to insure that you have written the affirmation correctly.

1. Is the goal one that you want personally? Is it exciting to you?

2. Did you place the time limit at least 30 days and no more than one year from todays date? Goals that are years in the future must be fragmented into objectives, that you can work on within the next year.

3. Did you begin with the word "I"?

4. Did you write the statements in the first person present or past tense? Be careful not to use future

tense such as, "I want to win the national championships or I plan to win the championships." Use, I am the national champion.

5. Did you write a statement describing the pay value to you for achieving the goal?

6. Did you write a statement detailing your plan to achieve the goal?

7. Did you repeat the goal statement?

Follow these guidelines and you will be able to write an effective Directive Affirmation for your goals.

CHAPTER FOURTEEN

"Become a Promoter"

My father told this story often about the cowboy in the bar. It seems that this cowboy was continually bragging to the bartender about the quality of his horse.

"My horse is the best looking, best trained, smartest animal In the state!" "I'd like to buy a horse like that. How much is he?" said the bartender. "Not for sale at any price. Everyone says he's the finest horse they have ever seen. I'm just proud to own him."

Finally the bartender could not stand it any more and offered the cowboy such a high price that a sale was made. The next day the bartender was furious, as he came into the bar.

"Where is the cheat, who sold me that horse. The animal is lame, ugly, untrained and worthless! You can't ride him. He's cross eyed and sway backed. What do you have to say for yourself cowboy?"

"I've just one thing to say....If you don't quit cutting down that horse, you ain't never gonna' sell him."

My favorite word in the English language is "promotion." The cowboy was successful because he was a good promoter. Webster defines promote as to raise or move forward to a higher or better position, to further the growth of something or to work actively, stirring up interest in an idea or concept. This is a powerful word.

A good mental manager is a promoter. I suggest three areas that we should promote.

1. Promote our systems.

2. Promote ourselves.

3. Promote the Self Image growth of others.

Promoting Systems

I am not an expert is politics, but I suggest that if we had a society filled with people promoting the country, instead of verbally tearing it down, we could achieve greater things as a nation. We must loudly champion the things that are right about our system, while silently going about changing the things that are wrong. Too many times, it is the other way around.

Athletes must promote their national associations and national governing bodies. We must promote our coaches, team administrators and managers. I spent twenty years as an athlete, ten of those years on the US national team. In the past eleven years, I have been a coach, teacher, administrator and a parent of athletes. I have gained a tremendous respect for those supporting sports activities. When I competed, I am certain that I was not always supportive of the people that ran the matches, the organizers or the administrators. I could not fully appreciate the difficulty of their tasks, until I had walked in their shoes.

Gold medals are never won alone.

If you are a parent of an athlete, I respect you for sacrificing for your children. I am the father of three. My boys are twins, both involved in shooting. When I buy equipment, I have to buy two sets of everything.

If you are a coach, I respect you for your diligence. When the team wins, everyone says "The athletes did it!" When it loses, they say, "It's the fault of the coach!" Most of the coaches I know are volunteers. Their only reward is the occasional praise they receive. They are never paid enough.

Finally, and most importantly, we must not forget the role played by the wives and husbands of the champions. The cost for an Olympic Gold medal is great, especially on the spouse. After winning my Gold medal, many people surrounded me at the functions, my wife and I attended. One day, I noticed that they had pushed Helen away from me. She was not seen as an important factor in the win. All they wanted was the medalist. I stopped the interview, joined my wife and held her close.

For the three years prior to my first Olympics, I spent more nights away from my family, than I did at home. Helen squeezed every penny out of our budget for extra ammunition. We never went on a vacation, we always took my vacation time at another rifle match. She did not complain. The Gold medal is ours, together.

Promoting Ourselves

It has become socially acceptable, in our society, to offer up ourselves as being less than acceptable when we speak to others. A few days ago, I heard a lady complement another, saying,"What a nice dress!" Her friend answered, "What, this old thing!"

You cannot expect people to think well of you, if you are not willing to think well of yourself. I am not saying that we should boast. But, I have had just about enough of people apologizing for being competent. I can assure you, that the Olympic champions that I know, do not hold their head down when a complement is offered. Do not be afraid of accepting the sincere praise offered by others.

Say out loud. "Thank You!" and silently, "That's like me!" The best way of promoting yourself is to make an effort to control your self talk. Say, "I am getting better at that!" instead of "I always do that poorly!"

You can promote inner growth by feeding your mind positive information through reading and listening. I encourage you to listen to tape recordings of motivational speakers, while you drive your car. Your local library is full of books on the subjects of positivity, personal growth and self improvement. Reading is a wonderful way to inherit the success of the writers. Make your mind a depository of positive information.

Promoting Others

Building Self Image, in others, is a primary task of parents, teachers and coaches. I offer six simple suggestions in promoting the self image others.

1. **Look them in the eye.** When you are speaking or listening to someone, you are building them up when you are looking right at them and tearing them down by looking away. Eye contact shows that you are concerned and that you place a high value on the person you are addressing.

2. **A name is everything.** Nick names can build up or tear down. Ask yourself, is this name aiding or hindering the student? How does the student feel about the name? If they do not value the name, do not use it.

Great care is taken when names are chosen at birth. Thirteen years ago, Helen and I selected, what we thought, was the most beautiful name, we had ever heard for a little girl. That is how our daughter, Heather Dawn got her name. When she was little, I called her "Heather-belle" and Helen called her "Doodle." Now, that she is growing up, "Doodle" just doesn't fit anymore. She will always be my Heather-belle, I just won't call her that in front of anyone.

3. Praise in public, correct in private. No one is motivated, by being chewed out in front of their peers. I see far too many coaches, guilty of this rule. This practice tears down self image. Public praise builds self image.

4. Praise twice as much as you correct. Remember, you are building by praising. There is no question that corrections must be made in a tactful, timely manner. But, you build Self Image by promoting more often than you criticize.

5. Never steal a dream or limit a goal. My twin sons, Brian and Troy are excellent soccer players. Last summer, we saw an advertisement in the newspaper about a five week, European/Soviet soccer tour. The team would play in seven countries, including the Soviet Union. Tryouts were to be held in San Antonio, Houston and Austin to select only sixteen boys from the state of Texas. When Brian, Troy and I arrived at the tryout, we discovered that the participants, once selected, would have to raise over $2500.00 each to offset costs. When these facts were announced, over seventy-five percent of the boys, walked off the field, before trying out. My sons came to me and said, "Dad, do you think we have a chance to make this team? Should we try out?" "You can't win if you don't enter!" I said. They both made the team. It was a tremendous effort, but both the boys raised their $2500.00 each from contributions made by the local merchants and businesses in our little town of Seguin. Their dream was realized. I am a very proud father.

6. Never give up on anyone. In the late 1950's and early 60's, the United States Army Marksmanship Unit shooters began to dominate international shooting. One of the shooters, in this formative period, spent his first three years on the Army team on the bench, unable to make the US national team. The Army questioned his ability. It appeared, he did not have what it took to become a champion. The shooter resigned from the Army, but returned to active duty within a year to make the 1964 US Olympic Team. That year Lones

Wigger Jr. won the Olympic Gold medal, with a new world record. Wigger is the most successful athlete, in international competition, in the history of this country. He has won more medals, made more US teams and set more world records than any American, in any sport. Some people choose their own time to become a champion. Do not give the appearance that you have given up on your students or children. Giving up on people, brings down the Self Image faster than any thing I know.

Become a promoter of your organization, of your self and of others.

Chapter Fifteen

"Answers!"

I realize that one of the deficiencies of a book is that you cannot ask the author a question. As I present seminars, I am frequently asked the same questions over again. I thought you might be interested in the answers to some of these questions about the Mental Management System.

Question # 1.

What should I do when problems occur?

When challenges occur in your attempt to achieve a goal, you must respond with appropriate and timely solutions. Most people view problems as obstacles, that keep them from their goals. I feel that problems and frustrations help me to identify the areas of needed growth. In this regard, problems are valuable. Also, they make us appreciate our successes.

Principle of MENTAL MANAGEMENT Number 10.

The Principle of Value: "We Appreciate Things in Direct Proportion to the Price We Pay for Them!"

I have noticed in my seminars that when students have their tuition paid by their sport associations, they are attentive and but rarely write anything down. When they pay their own tuition, they take good notes. People appreciate things in direct proportion to the price they pay for them.

People who have to struggle for many years to achieve their goal, appreciate the success even more. If you are experiencing some challenges in the journey toward your goal, this is not only quite common, but absolutely essential. Simply put, finding solutions to problems are essential to growth and provide a sincere appreciation of the accomplishment of the goal.

Question Number 2.

How many Directive Affirmations may I run at once?

The limiting factor in running a Directive Affirmation is the number of good key points you have available. You should not have more than one Directive Affirmation at a key point. If you can find ten key points then you may run two Directive Affirmations at the same time. I have never been able to run more than two at once.

Question Number 3.

How much time should I spend at a key point?

You should carefully read and visualize your Directive

Affirmation at each key point. In the first few days, this procedure may take two to three minutes at each key point. The time will shorten with practice. Soon, your Directive Affirmation will run automatically at anything that resembles your key point. If you have as a key point, your refrigerator, you may find that your Directive Affirmation will run as you approach any refrigerator.

Question Number 4.

When do I stop running the Directive Affirmation?

You must run the Directive Affirmation until your old Self Image is replaced by your new Self Image. Most people find a definite change occurring in Self Image within sixty days. Your job is not to Consciously try to achieve your goal. Your concern is only to run the Directive Affirmation. Soon, your Self Image will change and you will notice a corresponding change in your performance.

Question Number 5.

Were you nervous at the 1976 Olympics?

Yes! I have always gotten nervous in big competitions. I still get nervous before every seminar, I present. I suppose, I am the most nervous when I am watching my children in competition.

It is acceptable to be nervous before your competitions. In fact, I would become a bit worried if my students were not at least a little aroused, just before the Olympics. The key point here is:

It is permissible to be nervous before you perform, as long as you are not nervous as you perform!

I was not nervous while I was shooting on Olympic day. I used the Mental Management System. I reached the optimum mental level before I started shooting through Ultimate You Actual Rehearsal. I ran a Mental Program on each shot of the match and reinforced each good shot. I was not nervous while I was shooting. I had developed Sub-Conscious skill through a well designed training program. I had developed the kind of Self Image habits and attitudes that were consistent with winning the Gold medal. I was in the Triad State. You need not be nervous while you are competing, if you properly utilize the Mental Management System.

Question Number 6.

What did it feel like to win the Olympics?

When I remember the 1976 Olympic games I recall four separate emotional experiences.

1. Shooting the match was like walking on the edge of a knife blade, suspended like a bridge, over a canyon. I was behind my team mate, Margaret Murdock, for most of the match. We shot one hundred twenty shots in the Olympic three position match, forty in each of the prone,

standing and kneeling positions. At the end of the prone stage, Margaret lead me by a few points. Margaret is the best standing shooter, under pressure, I have ever faced. She turned in a miraculous performance standing. I performed well, but I was trailing her by five points going into kneeling.

I knew I had to shoot the best kneeling of my life to win. The weather was horrid. The wind was strong and tricky. I could make no mistakes in this position. I walked that knife edge, turning in the best kneeling of my life. When I had finished, I felt I had won the medal. I was not certain of Margaret's score, but I felt like the Gold medalist at that point. I had actually shot a 100 on one of my ten shot strings. I was especially proud of that.

2. Waiting for the official result was like aging ten years for every hour. International rifle shooting is not like the 100 yard dash, where the winner is immediately known. The scoring of the targets, in our match, took three hours to complete. The first set of scores put up on the results board are unofficial, pending protest. These scores are rarely changed. My score was the last to go up. Unofficially, Margaret had won the match by one point. I had another Silver. The reporters had been waiting for three hours. They wanted a champion to interview. They would wait no longer. Margaret Murdock was surrounded by reporters, I was alone.

I knew immediately that something was wrong, I have lost close contests before. I did not, at any time, feel like I had lost this match. I quickly looked up at the scores. They had made an error on my 100 kneeling score. It was scored a 99. That was incorrect. Several people had watched me shoot every shot, John Foster, Darrell Pace and my wife, Helen. All had scored that string a 100. A protest was called for. Another hour passed before the official and final results were posted.

3. Verification of a gold medal performance is always a positive feeling. The score keepers had incorrectly marked one of my tens, a nine. I was the Olympic Champion, but just as I had not felt a feeling of loss at the first score, I did not have a feeling of intense joy as the final score was posted. I could not help looking at Margaret. She had allowed herself to believe that she had won the medal. Now, it had been stripped away. We had equal scores, but under International Shooting Union rules, the tie was broken by the highest last ten shots. It was a bad rule. Either duplicate medals should have been awarded, or we should have had a shoot off for the Gold.

4. Finally, I remember the feeling of sharing. Every athlete in the Olympics yearns for the day when they are standing on the top step of the three tiered platform, while their national anthem is played. As the first notes of the

Star Spangled Banner were played, I brought Margaret up on the top tier. We stood together as the anthem was played. It was the only time this has happened in Olympic history. I did not feel complete, as the Olympic Champion, until Margaret joined me on that platform. As long as I live, that shall remain the most special of feelings.

Part V

"Learning More About the Mental Management System"

CHAPTER SIXTEEN

"Cease Firing"

A friend of mine is a fireman. He tells a story of a great apartment fire in the city. The fire spread so fast that the only way the people in the top floor could be saved, was to place a ladder from the roof to the window of an adjacent building. The people were forced to crawl across the ladder to safety. The ladder was ten stories from the ground.

Everyone was saved except a woman and her six year old son. The woman was afraid of heights, so the fireman, at the risk of his life, crawled across the ladder, rescuing her son. From the window the fireman called to the woman, "Come across now, the fire is close." She would not move. She kept looking down at the street below.

The fireman did the only thing he could have done, to save the woman. He took her son back across the ladder, to her. He said, "If your son is to live, you are going to have to save him!"

She did.

It was not like the woman to cross the ladder, but it was like her to save her son.

The time has come to wrap up. What do I hope you have learned from this book?

If a slow, short, uncoordinated kid can become Olympic champion, then it must be the mental and not the physical abilities that merit the medals.

Performance is a function of three mental processes: the Conscious mind, the Sub-Conscious mind and the Self Image.

Mental Management is the process of maximizing the probability, of having a consistent mental performance, under pressure, on demand.

There are ten Principles of Mental Management.

1. When the Conscious mind has a positive thought, it cannot, at the same time, be thinking negatively.

2. What you picture is critical.

3. The Sub-Conscious mind is the source of all mental power.

4. The Sub-Conscious moves you to do whatever the Conscious mind is picturing.

5. The Self Image equals Performance.

6. You can replace the Self Image you have with the Self Image you want and therefore, permanently change performance.

7. When the Conscious, Sub-Conscious and Self Image are balanced and working together, good performance is easy.

8. The more we think about, talk about or write about something happening, we improve the probability of that thing happening.

9. The Self Image can not tell the difference between what actually happens and what is vividly imagined.

10. We value things in direct proportion to the price we pay for them.

The **Mental Management Goal Setting System** is used to help determine the correct goal, plan and timetable for anything you desire to achieve. It's steps are:

1. Decide exactly what you want.

2. Decide when you want it.

3. List the pay value.

4. Ask "Why don't I have the goal now?"

5. Determine a plan to get the goal.

6. Ask "Is the prize worth the price?"

7. Schedule the plan.

8. Start now.

9. Never reach a goal without first setting another one.

10. Never, never quit.

Rehearsal is the most versatile mental tool and is used as mental practice, to control pressure and as contingency planning.

Running a Mental Program is composed of five points.

1. The point of Initiation.

2. The Point of Attitude.

3. The Point of Direction.

4. The Point of Control.

5. The Point of Focus.

Skills are developed by:

1. Catching yourself doing something right.

2. Training four or five days a week.

3. Where ever you are... Be all there.

4. Rehearse the match day within the training

session.

5. When you are performing well, continue.

6. Surround yourself with those that are superior to yourself.

Performance analysis is the champion's way of keeping a performance journal.

To change the Self Image one must:

1. Be willing to change.

2. Identify the habits and attitudes that you need to change.

3. Set up a new Self Image in conflict with the old one.

4. Exchange the old Self Image with the new one.

The most powerful tool in Mental Management is the **Directive Affirmation.** It has 8 steps.

1. Define the goal.

2. Set the time limit.

3. List the personal pay value of reaching this goal.

4. Outline the plan to reach the goal.

5. Write a Directive Affirmation.

6. Make five copies on cards.

7. Place the cards in prominent key points.

8. Read and visualize your Directive Affirmations daily.

We must promote our system, our self and others.

I have enjoyed sharing these thoughts with you. I wish you all the success you can imagine.

With winning in mind,

Appendix A

Directive Affirmation Example for
Building a Network

For those of you that are building a network marketing business, this it the Directive Affirmation that we use in our Amway group.

The Directive Affirmation:

Step 1. Define the goal...To add a new Direct Distributor leg to your organization.

Step 2. Set the time limit...Within 6 months of todays date.

Step 3. List the personal pay value of reaching this goal...

Each new distributor that you can help develop a $25,000 a year add on income, will generate over $10,000 a year in on going royalty income for you. Do this several times and you are financially independent.

Step 4. Outline the plan to achieve the goal.

A. Show the marketing plan to at least two new people a week in the leg.
B. Generate at least $200.00 in personal business each month.
C. Work in depth to find three leader legs.
D. Attend all the functions.
E. Read and visualize my Directive Affirmation daily.

Step 5. Write a Directive Affirmation.

12/1/89

"I have developed a new Direct Distributor leg in my organization. By helping a downline leader become a Direct Distributor and add an additional $25,000 to their income, I have added an additional $10,000 annually to mine. I have developed the new DD leg by showing the marketing plan at least two times a week in the leg, working in depth to find three leader leg, promoting and attending all the functions and reading and visualizing my Directive Affirmation daily. I have developed a new Direct Distributor leg in my organization.

Appendix B

Learning More about the Mental Management System

For additional copies of "With Winning in Mind, the Mental Management System" send $12.95 plus $2.05 shipping to Mental Management Systems. Volume discounts available for schools and teams.

Hear Lanny Bassham present the Mental Management System on Audio Cassettes.

1. Special New Course-Building Self Image in Competitive Youth for parents, coaches and teachers. Non shooting specific. 6 Tapes and a book for $69.00 plus $2 shipping.

2. The Mental Management Cassette Seminar for all Shooting Sports contains 8 audio cassettes plus a booklet. This recording of a "in person" seminar to archers, rifle, pistol and shotgun shooters has been newly revised and supplemented with studio recordings by Mr. Bassham. $89.00 plus $2 shipping and handling.

Video Tape Programs, VHS or BETA

1. Mental Management Seminar-3 videos for $119.00 plus $2.00 shipping.
Specify MMG for The Mental Management System on VideoTape 1 "Why Winners Win", Tape 2 "Tools and Techniques" and Tape 3" For rifle shooters ask for "Special Applications for Rifle Shooting", for pistol shooters ask for "Special Applications for Pistol Shooting" for archers and other sports & business ask for "Special Applications to Sport and Business"

2. Olympic Rifle Shooting-3 videos for $119.00 plus $2.00 shipping and handling. Tape 1 "The Fundamentals of Getting a Ten", Tape 2 "The Olympic 3 Positions and Air Rifle", and Tape 3 "Preparing for Competition."

Check, Mastercard and Visa orders accepted.

Send orders to:

Mental Management Systems
Dept. B
PO Box 225
Seguin, TX 78155

Appendix C

Join Lanny Bassham in Person.

"The In-Depth Individual Mental Management Seminar" A complete, one-on-one course of theory, tools and techniques designed to give the student the most complete program of Mental Management offered anywhere in the world. This seminar includes 19 hours of classroom and application training. A cassette series is included along with a one year consulting service to assure proper application of the techniques presented. Openings are extremely limited and all applications personally approved. Tuition available on request.

"The Two-on-One" Course – The same instruction as the in-depth course except two students are taught at the same time and the tuition is reduced. The one year consulting service is not included but may be added as an option.

"The One Day Mental Management Course" – A six hour seminar is presented including an overview of Mental Management and personal application. This is a one-on-one seminar with a cassette series included.

The One Day Mental Management Seminar can be presented to your group or school at your location by contract.

Custom courses are always available by contract. All courses are booked in advance by the remittance of 10% deposit. Financing of the in-depth course is available. Rooms and range use are available at the

International Shooting School, limited to availability.

For tuition and details write:

Mental Management Systems
Dept. B
PO Box 225
Seguin, TX 78155

Glossary

Mental Management is the process of maximizing the probability, of having a consistent mental performance, under pressure, on demand.

The Conscious Mind is the source of your thoughts or pictures. It can only think of one thing at a time.

The Sub-Conscious mind is the source of your skills and power to perform. All good performance is Sub-Consciously done.

The Self Image makes you "act like you" and is the sum of your habits and attitudes

In the *Traid state*, the Conscious, Sub-Conscious and Self Image are balanced and working together and good performance is easy.

Prediction is reinforcement in advance. It is an attitude that says. "I expect exceptional performance because you are an exceptional person."

Praise is reinforcement after the fact. It is an attitude that says. "I recognize exceptional performance because you are an exceptional person."

Rehearsal is mental practice.

Pressure is the stress you experience when you are in competition. It is composed of both fear and arousal.

Anticipation phase is what you think about immediately before you perform.

Action phase is what you think about as you perform.

Reinforcement phase is what you think about immediately after you perform.

Performance Analysis is a performance journal entry system that maximizes performance.

Directive Affirmation is a paragraph in the first person present tense that includes the goal, pay value and plan, that is used to change Self Image.

Key Point is a location for a Directive Affirmation card that you encounter often daily.

About the Author

Lanny Robert Bassham

Born in Comanche Texas, January second, 1947, the only child of William and Natalou Bassham.

Graduated, with a BBA in Management from the University of Texas at Arlington.

Served in the US Army for 9 years, highest rank held, Major.

President of Mental Management Systems, an international consulting firm in Mental Management.

Director of the International Shooting School, Seguin, Texas.

Lanny and Helen Bassham are Emerald Direct Distributors in Amway.